FROM
CAMPUS
TO
CORPORATION

AND THE NEXT
TEN YEARS

FROM
CAMPUS
TO
CORPORATION

AND THE NEXT
TEN YEARS

**By Stephen Strasser, Ph.D.
And John Sena, Ph.D.**

THE CAREER PRESS
62 BEVERLY RD.,
PO BOX 34
HAWTHORNE, NJ 07507
1-800-CAREER-1
201-427-0229 (OUTSIDE U.S.)
FAX: 201-427-2037

From Campus To Corporation And The Next Ten Years
ISBN 0-934829-69-1, $10.95

Copies of this volume may be ordered by mail or phone directly from the publisher. To order by mail, please include price as noted above, $2.50 handling per order, plus $1.00 for each book ordered. Send to: The Career Press Inc., 62 Beverly Rd., PO Box 34, Hawthorne, NJ 07507

Or call Toll-Free 1-800-CAREER-1 (in Canada: 201-427-0229) to order using your VISA or Mastercard or for further information on all books published or distributed by The Career Press.

Dedication

To Sarah, Joanne, Jeffrey, and Danny
To Sylvia, John Jr., Christopher, and Brian

Who have filled our lives
and our work with joy

Table Of Contents

Acknowledgements

AND NOTES TO
OUR READERS

Although **FROM CAMPUS TO CORPORATION and the Next Ten Years** has two authors, it could not have been produced without the assistance and encouragement of several people.

We wish to thank first our agent, Jane Jordan Browne, who has stood behind us and with us over the years. She is a wonderful person and advocate.

We also wish to thank Lee Bolzenius, Sherry Thomas, Barbara Balsley, and Sylvia Sena for their incisive comments, editorial suggestions, and moral support at all stages of this project. We cannot imagine undertaking such a project without them.

To Marshall Shearer, M.D., Phyllis Rose, Ph.D., and John Vaughn, J.D., we are indebted for guidance on psychological, behavioral, and legal issues. And to David Kolasky, Dick Dolan, and John Coleman, for suggestions on format and editorial matters.

Without the support of two individuals at The Career Press, this book would probably still be an idea rather than a reality: We are grateful to Ronald W. Fry and Tony Rutigliano for their vision, willingness to help, and editorial support.

We also wish to express our general indebtedness to The Ohio State University; its Colleges of Medicine and Humanities; to Professor Steven Loebs, chair of the Division of Hospital and Health Services Administration; Dr. Manuel Tzagournis, Dean of the College of Medicine; Professor Morris Beja, chair of the Department of English; and Professor Michael Riley, Dean of the College of Humanities.

Throughout **FROM CAMPUS TO CORPORATION**, we share with you observations of and conversations with numerous individuals, critical incidents that were reported to us, and surveys that we conducted. To protect the anonymity and confidentiality of all our sources, we have masked their identities. When necessary, we have altered their comments, without changing the meaning or intent of their words, to further protect their identities.

To insure anonymity and to clarify our presentation, we have at times provided a composite picture of workplaces, people, events, comments, and relationships. Any similarities you may observe to actual people, events, and relationships are purely coincidental.

Introduction

READY FOR AN EXCITING JOURNEY?

Job and career change, like death and taxes, are inevitable. Regardless of our ages, occupations, or status, all of us either are or will be caught up in the excitement, passion, anxiety, and frustration of change. Like it or not.

While job and career transitions exist throughout our working lives, perhaps the greatest, most rapid, and probably most *unexpected* occur during the first ten years after graduation from high school or college.

Presuming, therefore, that you fall somewhere *this* side of "thirtysomething," **FROM CAMPUS TO CORPORATION and the Next Ten Years** is written specifically for *you*. It is designed to help you understand and successfully manage the transition from student to employee and meet the numerous and varied demands of the workplace.

In other words, **FROM CAMPUS TO CORPORATION** will help you to *select* an appropriate job or profession, *obtain* the position that you desire, *overcome* the obstacles you will face at work, and *achieve* your full potential for professional and personal growth and development during the first decade of your career.

Rather than flying headlong into the job search, without even knowing what to expect, this book will help you predict and plan for changes in your work life, placing you in *control* of events instead of having events control *you*. Surprises are wonderful on your birthday. They're nightmares in the workplace.

FROM CAMPUS TO CORPORATION is several books in one:

It is a *resource* book filled with specific and concrete information on topics such as how to anticipate questions at an interview, how to create an effective resume, where to look for a job, and how to learn the culture of a firm.

It is a *guidebook* to help you avoid the shoals and maelstroms of the workplace, clarify your direction, and plan a future course.

It is a *"how to"* book that will help you evaluate yourself, solve work-related problems, develop your potential, and build a successful career.

Finally , it is a *personal* book that seeks to be supportive by listening to your concerns and speaking to you with candor, by encouraging you to see opportunity where you saw only limitation, by helping you achieve success where you expected only defeat.

We begin at the beginning—by helping you define your job or career interests in the first chapter and discussing the role of the "success equation" in selecting a type of employment. Once you have decided what you want to do, we help you to land your first job by describing how to create an effective resume and how to impress any prospective employer at a job interview.

Once you have selected an appropriate job—and we shall discuss how to weigh the various factors involved in making any job decision—we move to Step #2: helping you *succeed* at it. In two successive chapters, we discuss strategies for success during the first few weeks on a job and during the next ten years.

It is purely wishful thinking to believe (or to convince yourself) that once you have a job you will be immune from change and transition. The workplace is in a context flux; the only thing for certain is—that nothing is for certain.

"How do I know when I should look for another job?"
"What are the right and wrong reasons for leaving a job?"
"How do I know if I am doing well at work?" "How do I
manage a difficult boss?" "What do I do if I get fired?" "Is
working for a woman different from working for a man?"
"Should I date my colleagues?" "How will marriage affect
my work?" "How do I balance my personal life with my
professional life?"

These questions and dozens of others are addressed in the
second half of **FROM CAMPUS TO CORPORATION.**

Tests Aren't Only Given In School

Socrates espoused the first rule of education over 2000
years ago: "Know thyself." So while familiarizing you with the
nature of the transitions you are now facing and those which
you will encounter in the next ten years, we also will try to
help you understand yourself, your strengths and weaknesses, your predilections and aversions. Which is why you
will find, sprinkled throughout the book, diagnostic quizzes
and question-and-answer sections. These tests will allow you
to determine, for instance, if you are staying at your job for the
wrong reasons. Or your likelihood (if you are a male) of
having difficulty working for a female boss.

At other times, we shall try to hold a mirror up to you by
presenting interviews and case studies of people very much
like yourself facing the same problems you are currently
encountering.

The solutions we give to the myriad problems brought on
by looking for your first job and managing your career are
realistic and eminently "doable." These solutions, guidelines,
and recommendations reflect our collective experiences;
information gleaned from interviews with business executives, top- and middle-level managers and their subordinates,
and management specialists; and the professional literature
on human resource management.

You will immediately embrace many of our solutions and
recommendations. Others you will experiment with. Still

others you will probably reject. Hopefully, this process of evaluating the problems and issues you are facing and the ways in which you may react to them will force you to have a dialogue with yourself about the opportunities and difficulties brought on by these changes. Ultimately, you will be left with a deeper understanding of yourself, your colleagues, and your job or career.

Who Should Be Reading This Book

FROM CAMPUS TO CORPORATION is for a broad audience. It is relevant to anyone whose life is touched by work: students who are nearing graduation and looking for their first job and employees with a few years of experience under their belts; blue-collar, white-collar, starched-collar, and button-down collar workers; well-compensated middle managers and under-compensated teachers or social workers; those who *love* their jobs, those who *hate* their jobs, and those who simply wish they *had* a job.

FROM CAMPUS TO CORPORATION is also valuable, we believe, for your family and friends. The highs and lows of your working life will undoubtedly spill over into your personal life. And your family and friends will hear about it. From your recounting the day's events to railing bitterly against a boss or subordinate. From asking for feedback and advice to seeking a sounding board. From moodiness and depression to euphoria and exhilaration. From seeking support from family and friends to rejecting them in anger.

The more that your family and friends understand the nature and effects of the transitions which you're going through, the better able they will be to assist, advise, and support you as you go through them.

A person's career travels can be a cherished part of life. Join us in making that journey as positive, productive, and enjoyable as possible.

One

WHAT MR. CHIPS NEVER TAUGHT YOU

The transition from campus to corporation—or, as some prefer to describe it, from Miller Lite to Maalox—is one of the most dramatic, difficult, and disconcerting changes you'll ever have to make. Ironically, this overwhelming transition occurs at a time when you've had little (if any) experience in coping with *any* change, let alone understanding and adapting to the realities of the workplace.

Compared to the workplace, college is a relatively simple place for decision making. Success is easily defined—to earn an academic degree. Choices that must be made on the road to this "success"—the number and types of classes one must take, majors and minors, etc.—are minimal and simple.

Loyalties and allegiances are generally directed inward. Self-indulgent choices—"Would I rather get a tan or hear a lecture on Shakespearian sonnets?"—may be made without significant repercussions. Career goals and personal expectations are often defined in "Yuppie" terms: A house in the suburbs, BMW in the driveway, Rolex on the wrist, exotic vacations, 2.5 children. And all these activities are carried out in a secure atmosphere that protects aberrant personalities and unconventional lifestyles.

Little wonder that the transition to one's first career position is so difficult, for it is a transition that entails a host of radical changes—intellectual, emotional, and psychological—that strike to the very foundation of a student's psyche.

If high school or college life is fairly well mapped out for you, the workplace represents *terra incognita*—that area on old maps which was simply marked "Here There Be Dragons." Success *outside of school,* for instance, is an elusive concept whose definition undergoes periodic change and modification. The means to achieve it are even more varied, and decisions for advancing your career will have to be made on a frequent basis. Loyalties and allegiances are far less inner-directed—suddenly you must deal with loyalty to the Corporation, which may well mean supporting decisions and goals you've had absolutely no part in formulating (and with which you may even vehemently disagree).

Furthermore, conformity to these decisions and goals, as well as to a corporate code of personal behavior, are *expected,* and, for the most part, non-negotiable. Nor can you depend on having shared values with your colleagues—you will be required to interact—at work and socially—with a heterogeneous group of people who hold divergent views of the world.

The future is no longer a four-year span of time but an indefinite period extending beyond retirement. Finally, evaluation is ubiquitous—there is no refuge, no protective shield, no secure place to hide to avoid being evaluated in terms of your specific contributions to the organization.

The complexity of this particular transition need not cause fear and trembling. Transitions should be seen as opportunities to wrestle with exciting challenges and achieve personal growth. If you have not thought much about the changes that will occur as you replace your cut-off jeans and frisbee with a business wardrobe and briefcase, you are in good company. Be assured, however, that there *is* life after graduation, and that the guidance you need as you leave the warmth and security of the academic womb to enter the cold, scary world of the workplace is contained in this and the following chapters.

Let's Slay Some Dragons

Before dealing with specific methods of searching for, selecting, and adjusting to your first career position, there are a number of myths about career selection and job hunting that must be addressed, myths that create a barrier to succeeding at your first career transition.

MYTH 1: *"I must be absolutely certain that the position I select now is the right one for me. After all, if I am wrong, I'm forever doomed to a life of quiet desperation on the job."*

REALITY: This myth can stymie you before you even *begin* **your job search.**

It does not reflect the realities of the workplace as much as your own fears and anxieties—over making a mistake, facing the unknown, leaving the security of the academic world for the vagaries of the business world.

It is unlikely that your first job will be your last one. Nor will a job you find immensely satisfying today necessarily be the one you want to have ten years from now. As you grow professionally and personally, your priorities, value judgments, and career objectives will change often, sometimes radically. It is not uncommon to see teachers become entrepreneurs or engineers become business executives, for new careers to be undertaken after retirement, or for professional training to be sought in mid-life.

The tendency to switch jobs, according to virtually all predictions, will be *accelerated* in the future, with the average individual making as many as three *career*—not simply job— changes in his or her work life. While you should, of course, attempt to find the job most suitable for you, you must also remember that *no* career or job decision is forever, especially when it is your first one.

Rejecting this myth will allow you to keep your first transition in perspective and to form realistic expectations for yourself and your new job. Many people need time to find themselves and their careers—remaining flexible is crucial in this transition.

Finally, there is one suggestion to keep in mind: Draw a clear distinction between yourself and your work—your work is what you *do*; it is not what or who you *are*.

MYTH 2: *"I have heard that loyalty is everything when it comes to corporate success. This makes my first job decision even more important because if I leave within one year, I will be branded disloyal and opportunistic."*

REALITY: This myth is a variation of the first one. Do not *under*estimate the importance of loyalty to an employer, but do try to think of loyalty in broader terms.

Loyalty means giving your very best effort to an employer, supporting your boss and firm, taking responsibility for your actions, and genuinely caring about how well your firm functions. It does *not* mean being bonded to a firm in perpetuity.

Both firms and individuals change, often in unpredictable directions; sometimes the most loyal thing you can do is to *leave* a job. Successful people make wise, thoughtful decisions, not everlasting commitments simply for loyalty's sake.

MYTH 3: *"In selecting a career, I should never underestimate the importance of salary, opportunities for fast-track promotion, and geographical location."*

REALITY: Here's an easy trap to fall into!

We are a nation that admires glitz and glitter, that forces political candidates to hire image-makers, that continually ignores substance and applauds form. A career or job, however, should be chosen primarily for its content or substance.

This is the time to make an idealistic decision, one based on what type of work brings you pleasure, fulfillment, and growth. In making a selection, you may wish to be guided by your answers to two hypothetical questions:

"If I were independently wealthy and did not *have* to work, how would I spend my time?"

"When I retire and look back on my career, what would I most like to say I accomplished?"

The job that comes closest to answering these questions in a positive way is probably a good choice. The content of the job should be the number one criterion for selection. Swaying palm trees, lush offices, a fat salary, and a company Lamborghini are all tied for fourth.

MYTH 4: *"In selecting a career, I must make sure I choose the right industry."*

REALITY: The industry within which you work is important only to the extent that it allows you to perform the activities, do the tasks, and undertake the projects that you find challenging and fulfilling.

If you enjoy selling, for instance, focus on the opportunity to sell. *What* you sell is of secondary importance. Victor Kiam, III, president and chief executive officer of Remington Products and one of America's most accomplished salespeople, has, at various points in his career, sold bras, girdles, cosmetics, toothpaste, watches, and, of course, electric shavers. It was the wonderful, unadulterated world of selling —finding clients; identifying their needs; coaxing, cajoling, and persuading them; shaping their opinions; changing their mindsets; and closing the deal—that challenged and thrilled him. Let your job search be *interest*-driven, not *industry*-driven.

MYTH 5: *"My education trained me to do nothing practical, so I'd better take whatever job comes my way."*

REALITY: This myth reflects little understanding of the purpose of education mixed with one big dose of insecurity.

The purpose of education is to liberate you, to free you from your former limitations—allow you to undertake any manner of career, do any type of job, even ones that do not yet exist. So don't panic, and don't sell yourself short. You know and can do a lot more than you may think. If you have developed the ability to think logically, to analyze coherently, and to express your thoughts cogently and persuasively, you are qualified for the vast majority of jobs out there.

Whether you can prepare a capital budget, read a spreadsheet, create alternative life insurance packages, or understand the intricacies of foreign currency trading are, at this stage, secondary considerations. An astute employer will hire talent first, second, and third, *then* worry about teaching you the technical dimensions of a particular job. With the conceptual skills you have developed in school, learning the mechanics should be easy.

MYTH 6: *"I've gotten great grades, have strong letters of recommendation, and participated in a variety of extracurricular activities. I don't have to look for a job; the employers are out looking for me."*

REALITY: In a sense, this is the obverse of the last myth. If that myth was based on the failure to see your true strengths, this one is rooted in complacency, egotism, and smugness.

You are in a buyer's market, a condition that will not change in the near future. Hundreds of thousands of intelligent, hard-working, dedicated high school and college graduates enter the job market each year. The ones who actively and methodically prepare themselves are the ones who will have a better chance of achieving success in their first career transition. To do less is to hide your light under the proverbial bushel.

A subset of this myth is the belief that a career will find you—all *you* have to do is to lie in a hammock and wait. This attitude allows you to justify inertia and avoid taking responsibility for your life. It is also a convenient escape from the pain of failure, since if you do not try to influence events, you can avoid taking responsibility for the (inevitable) negative outcomes. In fact, this line of specious reasoning just allows you to rationalize failure. When you fail to find a job—and not looking for a job doesn't help your chances much!—you can always blame the heavens. But *you* know the gods had nothing to do with it.

Making a successful transition, now or at later stages of your career, requires numerous decisions. Perhaps the most important one is your resolve to take personal control of your life and to accept responsibility for the outcomes of your decisions—or lack of them. Sitting and hoping, fearing the future, dreading change, enjoying inertia, thinking wishfully, and avoiding accountability are elements in a zero-sum game... where you will always end up on the minus side of the scorecard.

The Success Equation

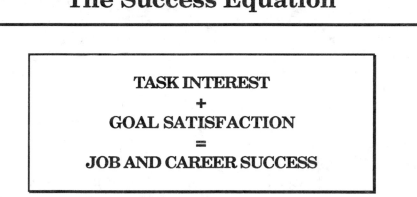

TASK INTEREST
+
GOAL SATISFACTION
=
JOB AND CAREER SUCCESS

Now that some of the rubble has been removed, you are ready to consider the basic elements in the Success Equation.

The first element is ***personal interest in the tasks***—the work—you will be doing. It is vital to select a type of work that you find exciting and fulfilling, that allows you to grow and develop professionally and personally, that will spark you to approach each day and each responsibility with enthusiasm.

Ralph Waldo Emerson suggested the importance of personal interest when he wrote 150 years ago that, "Nothing great was ever achieved without enthusiasm." Enthusiasm motivates you to rise early in the morning and work late at night, helps you cope with disagreeable colleagues or an indifferent boss, and permits you to overcome difficulties and problems instead of letting them overcome you.

In selecting a job or a career, your first allegiance should be to yourself. Your selection must meet your expectations and fulfill your dreams, not the expectations and dreams that others have for you. Nor should your selection be based on surface glitz and glamour. Separate the *accoutrements* of a job—a lengthy title, expense account, company car—from the *essence* of the position. What good is driving a wonderful car to see people you don't want to see, to discuss products you want nothing to do with?

Looking beyond surface attractions, however, is easier said than done. We spoke with Frank K., a recent graduate of a large Midwestern university, after he returned from a job interview in New York City. He bubbled with excitement over the beauty of the view from his office window and how wonderful the people were who interviewed him. When we asked him about the "content" of his job, his responses kept stressing the quality of his view and the lovely people he had met. He took the job, but his tenure was short-lived. Within a year he was back in the Midwest searching for another position, perhaps this time looking less at his office and more at what he would be *doing* in it.

The second element in the Success Equation is **goal satisfaction**. People who pursue challenging objectives and then achieve them are likely to have a high level of goal satisfaction. Goal satisfaction is both a process and an outcome—it is the result of the pleasure you derive from working toward a goal and the gratification you receive from attaining it.

The key is to be able to assess accurately your strengths and weaknesses, likes and dislikes, and predilections and aversions in a brutally honest fashion. You may find it useful to make a list of them and a list of the attributes, talents, and psychological factors required of a specific job, then compare the two lists. While the fit does not have to be perfect for a successful marriage, this method should identify jobs or careers that are not worth courting. Repeated person-job mismatches usually end in disaster.

Achieving job satisfaction also means avoiding jobs or careers that offer simple or shallow victories. If your goals are not challenging, they will soon become meaningless and, inevitably, fail to provide the desired satisfaction.

This notion may explain in part why some individuals who enter a family business in which success is virtually assured wind up frustrated, unhappy—and employed somewhere else. A stockbroker we interviewed, Ralph C., previously worked in his father's successful computer wholesale business. When we asked him why he left, he said that he wanted a career he could call his own, something he could look back on and say, "I built that myself." As we continued our conversation, he noted that he was having a terrible first year finding clients. In fact, after 11 months he ranked at the bottom in his firm in attracting new business.

But when we asked if he felt he had made a mistake in switching careers, he said, "Are you kidding? It's frustrating, especially when you're close to bringing in a new client and then it falls on its face. But I wouldn't go back to something as uninteresting as being a caretaker for my dad's moneymaker. I had no sense of accomplishment." Playing in a fixed card game may be financially profitable, but it builds neither self-esteem nor self-worth.

Virtually everyone knows someone who selected a seemingly appropriate career and achieved worthwhile goals but became dissatisfied with the work and, subsequently, with him- or herself. This may happen for a variety of reasons. Sometimes an individual becomes frustrated over the inherent limitations of his or her field. A social worker may become frustrated trying to help clients cope with seemingly insurmountable problems. A nurse may despair at being unable to help all of his or her patients recover from their illnesses. More often, an individual will simply no longer experience the psychological "high" or feeling of fulfillment after attaining a goal.

When such burnout occurs, the Success Equation suggests that you must act to regain your former interest and goal satisfaction. This may occur by simply examining the diversity within your profession and changing directions within the same field (e.g., moving from teaching to academic administration). It may necessitate a reassessment of your career expectations, or require you to take time off from work to become psychologically and emotionally refreshed. For some, it may require a more radical solution: You may decide that a complete change of career is necessary to reignite yourself. In any event, you will need to make an honest self-assessment and, if necessary, fundamental career changes.

Welcome To The Real World

Students are often so absorbed in the demands of their world—studying for exams, completing assignments, selecting appropriate courses—that they frequently fail to think of life beyond graduation until Commencement Day arrives.

The *good* news is that there is, indeed, life after graduation—an entire lifetime, in fact. The *bad* news is that specific preparation for a job or a career should begin at the outset of one's senior year, or even earlier.

Getting Started The Right Way—Early

Your senior year may become busier than you had anticipated, for it's time to add a new course to your class schedule—"Career Decision and Job Search 411"—which will necessitate, like its academic counterparts, a systematic approach, critical thinking, rigorous analysis, careful reading, and copious note taking.

First and foremost, it's time to determine precisely the activities that are of interest to you. Write down on a sheet of paper all of the tasks, projects, experiences, activities, hobbies, past jobs, academic courses, and sports that you find interesting, exciting, engrossing, or absorbing. Remove the blinders from your eyes, let your mind roam freely, and list EVERYTHING that you think you would enjoy.

For best results, expand this list over a period of several days. You may also wish to share your list with family and friends, for they may have insights into your character, temperament, and personality significantly different from your own. Your final list should be at least several pages long.

Your next task is to analyze the items on your list in an effort to find *patterns* or *themes* among them. You will probably find that some of the entries on your list fall into logical categories. You may have observed, for instance, that people often come to you for advice, and that you take pleasure in assisting them; that you enjoyed working as a camp counselor; and that you like tutoring individuals having difficulty in their classes. A theme that may be derived from these three experiences is an *enjoyment or delight in helping others solve their problems*.

The themes extrapolated from a list of activities one finds interesting or enjoyable may resemble the following:

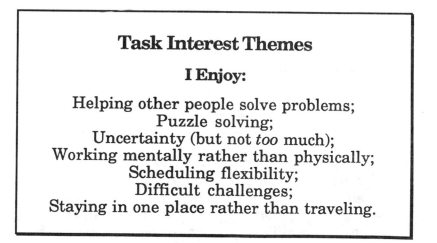

Task Interest Themes

I Enjoy:

Helping other people solve problems;
Puzzle solving;
Uncertainty (but not *too* much);
Working mentally rather than physically;
Scheduling flexibility;
Difficult challenges;
Staying in one place rather than traveling.

If you wish to delve deeper, ask yourself why these themes bring you pleasure. This will give you an even better understanding of where your job and career interests lie.

After you have identified the themes from your list, prioritize them, from most appealing or interesting to least. Since our likes and dislikes are rarely constant, keep your original list of activities and themes for future updating.

Next, place each theme on a separate piece of paper. Then brainstorm for any type of job that reflects each "activity theme." Ask family, friends, and job and career counselors to suggest jobs that they believe reflect the various themes you have extrapolated. If, for instance, in the hypothetical example above, we gave the highest ranking to the first theme, our list of jobs or careers may resemble the following:

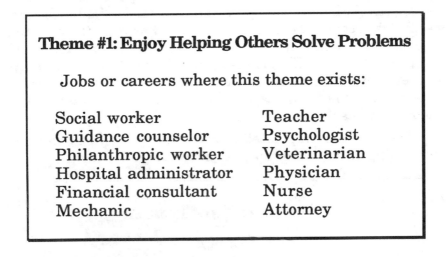

Theme #1: Enjoy Helping Others Solve Problems

Jobs or careers where this theme exists:

Social worker   Teacher
Guidance counselor   Psychologist
Philanthropic worker   Veterinarian
Hospital administrator   Physician
Financial consultant   Nurse
Mechanic   Attorney

Identifying Goal Satisfaction

As we noted in the Success Equation, task interest should be accompanied by goal satisfaction. Both parts of the equation are generally necessary for success. Thus, you must now examine each of these potential jobs in terms of its significance for you and your ability to perform it successfully. The nursing profession, for instance, may be on your list, but you realize that you have no aptitude for the natural sciences, or you may fear that you will identify too closely with those who are ill, or you may simply faint at the sight of blood.

Ask yourself which jobs on your list *feel right* or do *not feel right* to you. Is being a physician or a mechanic something that you can see yourself doing for the foreseeable future?

Does the thought of pouring over numbers and fiscal data seem more or less attractive than root canal?

Cross off those jobs for which you are obviously intellectually, emotionally, or temperamentally ill-suited, and highlight those that seem to fit your abilities, personality, and temperament. Our objective at this point is to *shorten* the list by removing jobs that are patently inappropriate for you. Since you have just begun your job search, it is likely that you may not have sufficient information about a specific job to know if it is inappropriate or not. When this happens, highlight that job and keep it on the list for further research.

Researching Jobs and Careers

After you have narrowed your list to several jobs, your next task is to learn as much as you can about these types of employment. The job placement or career counselors at your school are a valuable resource for job information. They will be able to provide you with information on work settings, specific job responsibilities, salary ranges, desirable personal qualities, opportunities for advancement, projected demand for new employees, as well as a general analysis of the pros and cons of the jobs you are considering. They may also be able to help you narrow your "short job list" further by describing how specific jobs or careers match the themes you have prioritized.

One particularly effective means of learning more about a job is to talk to people already working in that field, an exercise that will quickly replace romantic illusions with the realities of the work-place. You may find these individuals among your own network of friends and acquaintances, your family's network, or from names provided by job placement or career counselors. Before talking to people in a field you are thinking of entering, prepare a good list of relevant questions, such as:

1. What do you like most about your job?
2. What do you like least about your job?

3. (If autonomy is important to you) To what extent are you permitted to make decisions on your own?

4. (If economic security is important to you) What are the prospects for this field and for employment in the future?

5. (If family life is crucial to you) Does one have to work 14 hours a day, or does one have time for a full personal and family life?

6. (If you value a variety of assignments) Do you tend to repeat the same tasks, or are you regularly given various assignments?

7. (If working with others is important to you) Do you generally work alone on projects, or do you frequently interact with others?

Listen actively to what your interviewees say. Take notes on their responses and on the feelings you are experiencing from what you hear and see. Do not be afraid to ask a question that you think may sound foolish *if it is a question that you do, indeed, want answered*. And don't be afraid that your questions will reveal too much about yourself—you are there to gain all the relevant data that you can.

In addition to asking questions, observe your interviewees and their surroundings carefully. Do they seem bored, jaded, or uptight? When they talk about their job responsibilities, are they excited? Do they smile very often? Do you find the general ambiance of the office emotionally comfortable?

To increase the reliability of your information, interview more than one person. After several interviews you may find that opinions about your suitability for a particular job are starting to form. Before allowing those opinions to solidify into a final decision, however, gather additional information.

An excellent way to learn more about a specific job or area of work is to obtain an internship. Your career counselor can apprise you of internships available for either academic credit or salary (sometimes both) in virtually all major fields of employment. The hands-on experience offered by an internship is an excellent way to determine if a specific job or career is compatible with your talents, interests, and values.

Besides giving you practical knowledge of a field, an internship will also help you avoid the Catch-22 situation often faced by people looking for their first job: You can't be hired because you lack work experience. An internship will *give* you that experience, while also getting your foot in the organizational door by demonstrating your talents and maturity to a prospective employer.

Reading about various jobs and careers can also help you make an appropriate decision. Your job placement or career counselor may be able to recommend books or pamphlets on the jobs or careers you are researching. Take notes on those aspects of a job that are of greatest interest to you—e.g., job availability, projections of future growth in the field, educational requirements, desirable personal characteristics.

Sorting It All Out

At this point you probably will have accumulated a mountain of data. It is now time to analyze this material from the standpoint of task interest and goal satisfaction. Strip away the surface and superficial aspects of a job. Go to its very core and ask yourself if this type of work captures your *interest*, has a *meaningful* purpose, and is *consistent* with your talents, abilities, needs, desires, and values.

You may, at times, feel confused and unsure of yourself. That goes with the territory. But we hope that you are also excited because of what you have learned about potential jobs and careers and about yourself.

We hope you are excited about the prospects of meeting new people and working in a new environment, of undertaking a job that you will find challenging and fulfilling.

Finally, we hope that you enjoy a sense of personal control knowing that *you* and *not* the vagaries of luck or the marketplace are driving your career choices.

Two

FURTHER INTO
TERRA INCOGNITA:
THE RESUME

The first stage in presenting yourself to any potential employer is to create an informative, well-written, and attractive resume.

To understand the function of a resume, you may want to borrow an analogy from the marketplace. You are selling a product—yourself—to a buyer. The resume is your advertising. If the buyer finds the advertising sufficiently stimulating and interesting, he or she will want to learn more about the product—you—and arrange an interview.

The function, then, of a resume is limited yet important. It does not *secure* a job for you *per se,* but rather introduces you to employers and attempts to convince them to invite you for job interviews, during which securing a job *is* a possibility.

"Where Do I Begin?"

You begin by making lists. Take separate sheets of paper and type at the top of each sheet the various headings discussed below. You may cut material later, but you need to start with comprehensive, exhaustive lists.

Educational Background

In this section, include all of the institutions you have attended and the diplomas or degrees you have earned. Include the full name of your degree, its initials, the area in which you majored, and the dates you attended school—e.g., 1985-89, Bachelor of Science (BS) in chemistry, The Ohio State University, Columbus, Ohio.

A frequent mistake is to omit special training you have received or certification you have earned that may help you get an interview. If you are a nurse and fail to record your state licensure number, a personnel director may assume that you are *not* yet licensed or that you have not passed the appropriate state examination. If you fail to list that you have earned an ACSW (Academy of Certified Social Workers) certificate, you may have screened yourself out from obtaining a supervisory position.

Continuing education courses, relevant workshops, and formal seminar work should also be included in this section. An automobile mechanic should list specialized training—Certificates in Transmissions, Electrical Systems, Air Conditioning, etc. A secretary should list seminars attended to learn multiple types of computer software, such as WORD-PERFECT, D-base, and Lotus.

This is no time to hide your light under a bushel—you want your resume screener to know all the job-related training you have had.

Work Experience

List, in reverse chronological order, all the jobs you have held, including summer jobs, part-time employment, and volunteer work. For each work experience, list the dates you held the job, your formal job title, the company or organization for whom you worked, and its address. After that, write a few short sentences (no more than the equivalent of three or four typed lines) describing what you did in each position.

For example: 1988-1989, Sales Assistant. The Yuppie Clothing Store, 1656 Job Street, Los Angeles, California 93213. Responsibilities included: Sold men's "everyday wear," conducted quarterly inventory, assisted manager in merchandising clothing, managed customer complaints, and audited cash receipts and day-end sales.

The resume reader would know after reading 36 words the breadth of your experience in sales. He or she has learned that you not only sold, but that you also had the maturity and expertise to assist in merchandising, the diplomacy to manage irate customers, and the trustworthiness to handle cash and financial recordkeeping.

Academic and Work Achievements

"Achievements" represent, in the parlance of the workplace, "outcome measures," or demonstrable evidence of the quality of your work and academic performance. Merely saying that you earned a degree or that you worked for a firm does not tell the resume reader very much about the *quality* of your work at school or on the job. Compare the following, and ask yourself which resume writer is more likely to be granted an interview:

Writer A: Worked successfully at Widget Company.

Writer B: Worked at Widget Company. Saved firm $2,000,000 annually by lowering accounts receivable from 69 days to 22 days.

Writer A: Graduated with a BS.

Writer B: Graduated with a BS in chemistry (GPA 3.30); awarded the Kiwanis and Ashland Chemicals scholarships

Writer A: Had an excellent sales year in 1989.

Writer B: Exceeded sales quota by 21% in 1989.

Writer A: Worked for two years at The Bells & Whistle Company.

Writer B: Worked for two years at The Bells & Whistle Company; received two merit salary raises and two letters of commendation from my supervisor.

The strength and persuasiveness of Writer B's resume lies in its specific, concrete, and quantitative indicators— "hard outcome measures"—of his or her performance. While the reader may have a general and vague sense of the achievements of Writer A, the magnitude and significance of the accomplishments of Writer B are immediately apparent. Furthermore, numbers ($2,000,000), percentages (21% above quota), and facts (GPA: 3.30) catch the resume reader's eye.

Honors and Awards

Resume writers, unfortunately, often fail to include honors and awards, but *you* shouldn't. Honors and awards reveal much job-related information about you: You are competitive, dedicated, tenacious, willing to work hard, and have high standards. And these traits have been noticed by others.

Make this list as complete as possible, including items such as commendations, contests and competitions that you have won or in which you have performed well, nominations for offices or positions, elections to offices, scholarships, and tributes of any type. Some of these items will overlap with your list of academic and work achievements.

A measure of redundancy is acceptable, even beneficial, for it will reinforce what you have said earlier. You may, however, want to vary the form of presentation. If, for instance, you earlier placed "cum laude" after your academic degree, you may now want to list the specific quarters or years you were on the Dean's List.

A typical list of honors and awards may resemble the following:

1989 Voted "Most Inspirational Team Member" on varsity soccer team;

1988 Received honorable mention for "Tournament Team," NCAA regional soccer tournament;

1988 Elected junior class vice-president;

1986 Awarded the Philmore Scholarship for excellence in science ($4,000 for tuition);

1985 Received community service award for commitment to overcoming illiteracy in Upper Arlington, Ohio;

The importance of listing a variety of honors and awards, even ones that are not directly job-related, may be seen in an interview we had with Richard M., an oil company executive. He had mentioned on his resume that he played for one year on the professional tennis satellite tour. About twenty minutes into his job interview, the questions turned from oil to tennis. The three interviewees loved hearing about the travails of a rookie on the tour: qualifying for events at 7:00 on Sunday mornings, sitting on your thumbs for a week after losing in the first round, earning a whopping total of $281.17 for an entire year.

Although his educational and professional training in management were excellent, he is convinced that "a key to the success of my interview was talking about my experience on the satellite tour. I think it made them see me as an individual and not just another manila folder. They seemed to take me seriously as a goal-directed person."

Be sure to provide a brief explanation of any awards and honors that are not self-evident.

Writer A: Received the 1989 James A. Genius Scholarship.
Writer B: Awarded the 1989 James A. Genius Scholarship, a competitive scholarship for excellence in interior design.

By defining the nature of the scholarship and the basis for the award, Writer B's statement is clearer and more persuasive than Writer A's.

Skills

Whether you realize it or not, you have accumulated a variety of skills from a variety of sources—school, job experience, community activities, organizational involvement, even hobbies. List these skills on a separate sheet of paper. If, for instance, you are a computer buff, you may possess a number of proficiencies:

Computer Skills

- Programming skills in: COBOL, Fortran, Pascal, Assembler, Job Control Language;
- Software design;
- Lotus 1-2-3 and spreadsheet applications;
- Statistical packages (SPSS, SAS);
- WORDPERFECT, Wordstar, and Nota Bene.

If you were a business major or worked in an accounting office, your list of fiscal skills may resemble the following:

Finance/Accounting Skills

- Capital budgets;
- Economic feasibility studies;
- Cost benefit and cost effectiveness analyses;
- Cost accounting systems and design;
- Lotus 1-2-3 and spreadsheet applications;
- Management information systems design and implementation.

To determine your skills, begin with broad job-related categories such as "General Management Skills," "Writing Skills," "Technical Skills," "Presentational Skills," "Interpersonal Skills," and fill in the specifics.

If some of these skills have not appeared on your lists of "Educational Background" and "Work Experience," you should integrate them into those sections. If your level of description in "Educational Background" and "Work Experience" will look too cluttered, you may wish to include a "Job-Related Skills Inventory" as a separate section of your resume. The only rule we urge you to follow is: *Always* let the resume reader know what *you* know.

Personal Interests & Extracurricular Activities

One of the inherent weaknesses of the resume format is that it stresses facts and, as a result, fails to create a holistic picture of an individual. A section on your "personal interests" will help to reduce this deficiency. This is probably the only part of your resume that will suggest the person—your attitudes, values, beliefs, interests—behind the data.

Once a prospective employer is convinced that you possess the needed skills and experience for a job, the hiring decision is often based on what kind of a person you are. Personal interests and activities can help him or her get a better sense of that. Noting on your resume, for instance, that you contribute time to community service projects, such as Big Brothers or Big Sisters of America, would suggest to a prospective employer that you possess a social conscience and are sensitive and responsive to community needs.

Mentioning that you are involved in competitive sports or that you play the guitar for a musical group would indicate that you have the ability to set goals and the tenacity and discipline to achieve them. Listing class and organizational offices you have held—"Associate Editor (Features), College Newspaper"—would suggest you possess strong interpersonal skills and leadership qualities.

Another reason for listing your interests may be found in the example of Debbie B., a recent graduate with a degree in English from a large Midwestern university. She gave her resume to a university career counselor for review. He asked her if she had any hobbies or personal interests that could be included. With a combination of bashfulness and embarrassment, she sheepishly said that she was very interested in sewing (one is led to assume by her reaction that this is a skill not held in high esteem these days on university campuses). She followed the recommendation of the counselor and listed various types of sewing on her resume as her primary hobby.

At the risk of making a short story long, she is now employed as an editor at a trade magazine covering the sewing and needlecrafts industries. It may well be that the one element that distinguished her from the legions of other English majors who applied for the job was her specific and appropriate personal interest.

The personal interests and extracurricular activities section should appear toward the end of your resume, immediately before you list your references or recommenders.

References

If the primary purpose of a resume is to secure an interview, then the names, titles, addresses, and phone numbers of your references, placed on the last or a separate page of your resume, may help to achieve that objective.

It is very possible that the names of some of your references will be recognized by a prospective employer as respected members of a given field, in which case there is an increased likelihood of your being granted an interview. While we do not subscribe to the old, cynical adage—"It's not what you know, but who you know"—the importance of professional networking, of having worked or studied with an individual well known in a field, should not be dismissed. When candidates with similar credentials apply for a job, employers are more likely to select for an interview individuals whose recommenders are familiar to them. Although name recognition may be helpful, the content of a letter of recommendation is still its most important dimension.

When asking your references for permission to use their names, update them on your progress in school and your career aspirations. Give them a copy of your resume so that their recommendations may contain specific, concrete information about you and reflect a degree of personal familiarity with your work and achievements.

Setting Up Your Resume

You have just finished assembling the raw material of your resume. The only problem is that the information is scattered over numerous "Resume Topic Sheets." It is now time to bring order out of chaos, to create an honest, clear, concise, visually appealing brochure about yourself.

Prioritizing

If you have done your job properly, you have probably listed more information about yourself than can possibly fit into a resume shorter than a thesis. Go through your data sheets and cross off items that you believe you will not have space for in your resume, regardless of the job for which you are applying. Next, indicate with a highlighter information that you believe *must* be included in your resume.

Since a resume should be tailored for a specific job, you may want to produce two or three versions of your resume. Mark those items on your Resume Topic Sheets that you think may be useful for various types of jobs. If, for instance, you are applying for a coaching position, you will want to emphasize your involvement in athletic and youth programs. If you are applying for a job in sales, you will want to stress your ability to interact with people and your public speaking skills.

Organizing

Generally, the first two sections of your resume should be "Educational Background" and "Work Experience." But put your best foot forward—if your work experience is better than your educational preparation, list it first.

If your job skills are extensive, you may wish to list your skills inventory first, then follow with your educational background and work experience. If you do not place them in a separate section, then integrate your job-related skills into your educational background and/or work experience.

Your academic and work achievements should be integrated into the first two sections, "Educational Background" and "Work Experience."

The third major section should generally be "Awards and Honors;" the fourth section, "Personal Interests and Extra-curricular Activities;" and the final section, "References."

Length

"Thou shalt not create a resume longer than one page" has somehow become the Eleventh Commandment. This notion forces applicants to cramp three pages of legitimate, informative material into a one-page resume that looks like the twenty-third Psalm written on the head of a pin.

A resume should never be padded. Prospective employers *read* resumes; they don't tend to *weigh* them. But if you have relevant experience, achievements, honors and awards, training, or education that may increase your chances of being invited for an interview, don't hesitate to exceed a page.

If your resume exceeds *four* pages—which would be fairly remarkable if this is your first job after graduation—you may wish to preface your full-blown resume with a one-page "Summary Resume." The summary should be designed to whet the job screener's appetite—to highlight your most significant and interesting accomplishments—so that he or she will want to partake of the larger feast.

Visual Appearance And Layout

An effective resume is visually appealing and easy to read. We recommend that you design your resume on a word processor so that you will have flexibility in editing, reordering material, and using various printing fonts.

To visualy draw the reader's attention to your accomplishments, list material in short sentences or sentence fragments. Avoid entries that exceed four single-spaced, typed lines. Large blocks of text, like the one below, may contain important material but appear uninviting and overwhelming to the reader.

Job responsibilities included: Designed mail and telephone interview surveys. Pretested the surveys and made revisions. Conducted one hundred one-on-one interviews with research sample. Coded and keypunched survey research data. Verified statistical software computer programs used to analyze data. Analyzed survey data using the following statistical analytical techniques: a. Regression; b. Analysis of variance; c. Chi-squared. Drafted fifty-page feedback reports to clients. Presented survey results to clients.

This entry would intimidate all but the most courageous resume reader. The writer has amassed a great deal of information, but it is presented in a confusing and inaccessible manner. The reader would be well-advised to drop bread crumbs along the way to keep from becoming hopelessly lost.

Furthermore, the entry fails to differentiate among the various items; the material is not visually broken into small, salient, and more readable sub-units. Here's the same information presented in a much more readable and comprehensible fashion:

Job Responsibilities Included:

- Designed mail and telephone interview surveys;
- Pretested surveys and made revisions;
- Conducted 100 one-on-one interviews with research sample;
- Coded and keypunched survey data;
- Verified statistical software computer programs used to analyze data;
- Analyzed survey and interview data with following statistical analytical techniques: Regression; Analysis of Variance; Chi-squared;
- Drafted 50-page feedback reports to clients;
- Presented survey results to clients.

Clarity and differentiating among items may be achieved through a variety of methods: indenting and offsetting, blocking text, underlining, **boldfacing**, *italicizing*, s-p-a-c-i-n-g, numbering, CAPITALS, bullets (•), and crosses (+). Typographical changes can help highlight key aspects of your credentials for the reader's attention. Variety is not only the spice of life, it also makes for visually appealing and effective resumes.

Proofreading

Work Experience: Cheek-Out Clerk, Bun's Drug Store, Columbus, Ohio—worked seperate shifts, morning and night.

Creating an effective resume takes time and effort. Yet the time and energy you have expended may be undercut by a resume that contains misspellings and typos. Carefully proofread your resume, and then ask several others to proof it. You probably caught the typo "Cheek," but how about "seperate?"

The Cover Letter

You should not send out a resume without a cover letter accompanying it. There are three basic rules for writing an effective cover letter:

Rule 1. Keep it short—no more than one-half page in length, single-spaced. Resist the urge to repeat your entire resume.

Rule 2. In the second paragraph mention one or two of your trump cards—one or two aspects of your education, experience, skills, and/or achievements that you believe make you eminently qualified for the job.

Rule 3. Indicate in the last paragraph that you would like to have an interview, and when you will call or write to check the status of your job application.

The sample cover letter on page 41 may help you write your own.

The cover letter is also the appropriate place to indicate any unusual method you have employed in organizing the material of your resume. If, for instance, your resume is very long, and you have decided to write a one-page summary resume, followed by the full-blown version, or if the first page of your resume is a skills inventory, inform your reader of this in the cover letter.

Recordkeeping

It is advisable at this point to create a filing system for your job search, including at the very least the following categories:

- *Company contacts:* The names of individuals to whom you have sent your resumes and the dates on which they were sent, phone calls that have been

Sample Cover Letter

1150 Easy Street
Eldorado, Ohio 43210
January 5, 1990

Mr. Ralph Job
Vice-President, Human Resources
Rockwell Industries
Columbus, Ohio 43220

Dear Mr. Job:

I am a senior at Midwest State University, and I would like to be considered for a position as computer programmer with Rockwell Industries.

As indicated on my enclosed resume, I am a computer science major. Last summer I worked for The Battelle Research Institute, where I assisted in the design of a simulation computer program for F-14 fighter plane training.

I would appreciate the opportunity to speak with you about my academic background and professional experience. If you wish additional information, please feel free to call me at 459-0768. I shall telephone you in two weeks to inquire about the status of my application.

Sincerely,

made to personnel directors, interviews granted and denied, and your current status with each company.

- **Contacts/networking:** People to call, job leads given to you.

- **Job-search telephone directory:** Easily accessed telephone numbers you have accumulated pertaining to any job possibility.

- **Newspaper and trade journal ads** to which you have responded or intend to respond.

- Copies of various **job-specific resumes** and their cover letters.

Organizing the plethora of information involved in a job search will help you to avoid embarrassing mistakes, such as responding to the same ad twice, calling a prospective employer for an update two days after you sent your resume, sending the wrong resume to the wrong company, or erroneously thinking that you sent out a resume to a certain firm when you didn't.

10 Tips To Improve Your Resume

1. Use forceful verbs whenever possible to give your resume strength and vitality—e.g., "generated," "created," "made," "developed," "implemented," "restored," "elected," "awarded," "appointed."

2. If you have financed your education, definitely mention it: "Financed 75% of all educational expenses through employment while in school."

3. List your grade point average, if it's good. If you are in a difficult major, compare your grade point average to the mean GPA in the department or college.

4. Resist any urge to be cutesy. Starting the cover letter with, "Hi, I'm Ralph Blowhard, and guess what? Your hiring problem is over;" or "If you

think Shakespeare was good, wait till you see my copy;" or including drawings of Smurfs generally do not have the effect that their authors intended.

5. Do not enclose your picture. One human resource manager we spoke with indicated that she tries very hard to follow Equal Employment Opportunity guidelines, and that a picture only makes her job more difficult. Unless the information is related to a job activity, do not indicate your age, race, sex, or religious preference.

6. In general, we recommend that you not include a statement of your career objectives in the resume proper. Such statements often border on cliche and wheel-spinning—"I am looking for a progressive company;" "I desire meaningful work;" "I want to reach my fullest human potential."—and are probably not worth the valuable space they take up.

   If you feel *compelled* to include a statement of career objectives, place it in your cover letter and be certain that it is succinct, to-the-point, and devoid of hackneyed sentiments.

7. Be sure to include your address and phone number (we sometimes overlook the obvious). If you will not be at that telephone number very often, then list an alternative number where you can be reached or invest in an answering machine.

8. Write pithy, short sentences or sentence fragments. Avoid the temptation to explain activities in minute detail.

9. Have your resume printed with a laser printer on high-quality paper. Avoid at all costs printing your resume on a dot matrix printer.

10. Be truthful, no matter what. Lying or fabrication on a resume can be grounds for dismissal. According to one recent study, approximately 33% of job applicants falsify information; a 1987 study reported by the *Columbus* (OH) *Dispatch* reported that *up to* 67% misrepresent or fake information. That so

many applicants do this is in no way a justification for *your* doing it. It is unethical and surely not worth the inherent risks.

Where To Send Your Resume

There are several basic ways to acquire the names of firms or individuals to whom you may wish to apply for employment.

Word of mouth is one of the best ways to identify potential employers. Go public! Let family members and friends know you are on the job market and that you desire work in a certain field. Ask them for the names of appropriate firms or individuals. View everyone you meet as a possible source for a job lead.

Ask the career or job placement counselor at your school for the names of appropriate firms or individuals.

Read employment-opportunity ads in your local newspaper, in newspapers from communities in which you wish to work, and in the *Wall Street Journal's National Employment Weekly.*

Contact individuals already working in the industry you wish to enter and ask them how to identify job possibilities. If you are interested in the insurance industry, for instance, ask an insurance agent if there is a national or regional clearing house that publishes a job list. Inquire if there is a job placement session at national or regional insurance conventions

Ask your local librarian for career directories in the field you wish to enter.

Contact your alumni association for employment lists or the names of former graduates in the field you wish to enter.

Write to firms for which you've daydreamed about working.

Contact your local Chamber of Commerce. Many publish employment directories, including brief descriptions of companies in your area and the names and addresses of their personnel directors.

Ask your priest, minister, or rabbi, as well as individuals in social, civic, or sports organizations to which you belong for the names of appropriate firms or individuals.

Use the Yellow Pages to identify appropriate local firms.

The days after you send your resume to a potential employer will seem to pass slowly. You will suddenly become acutely aware of the precise time of the day that your mail is delivered. Do not lose confidence in yourself, in the quality of your accomplishments, or in your ability to earn employment. You have taken important first steps: You have selected a type of work that you believe you will enjoy, and you have prepared an effective and attractive resume.

It may not happen today. It may not happen tomorrow. But it *will* happen—you will receive a letter or a telephone call from a potential employer asking you to come for an interview.

Before going to that interview, however, make sure you have read the next chapter.

Three

HERE THERE BE DRAGONS: THE JOB INTERVIEW

If you have created an effective resume and have the appropriate qualifications for a job, you will probably be invited for an interview.

The interview is a crucial step in a job search, for it usually represents the first meaningful verbal interaction between you and your potential employer.

We understand that you may feel nervous and desperate, and that you would like to say, "Give me this job, or else I will slash your tires." We do not recommend this strategy. Your interviewer may have taken the bus.

What Interviews Want To Know

In a very real sense, a successful interview begins before you ever set foot in the interviewer's office—with your preparation for this face-to-face appraisal. Part of that preparation should be to anticipate the questions that you will be asked and to plan effective and persuasive answers to them. Off-the-wall questions—"If you were a car, what would your hubcaps look like?"—are, thank God, a rarity. This type of preparation is not unlike studying for an exam in which the instructor distributes beforehand a list of questions on which you will be quizzed.

Before preparing answers to potential questions, however, it is helpful to know why interviewers ask the types of questions they do.

Why do interviewers ask anything at all? They are trying to discover:

- Whether you possess the *technical skills and abilities* to perform a job effectively. So some questions will concern your training, work experience, and ability to handle equipment or difficult situations.

- Whether you represent a *good person-job fit.* Determining this often goes beyond evaluating your skills and ability. The interviewer will, for instance, ask questions aimed at assessing your attitudes, personality, and behavior patterns, such as your tolerance for stress, your willingness to adapt to new situations, your desire to reach a goal.

- Your *interpersonal skills.* Most jobs involve working with others and/or dealing with the public. In both cases, your ability to listen carefully and empathize with others and your sensitivity to cultural, racial, and gender differences are important.

- The *evidence* to support statements you have made in your resume or which your recommenders have made about you. Thus you will be asked to give illustrative examples or specific instances which demonstrate the strengths and talents you and your recommenders have mentioned.

- Your *level of commitment* to your profession and to his or her company. Questions pertaining to how you became interested in this line of work, where you wish to be in five years, or what direction you wish your career to take are generally designed to elicit this information.

- Your *leadership style* and approach to workplace problems. Do you lead by example or by command? When confronted with a problem, do you prefer to call a meeting of those concerned or seek a solution on your own? Are you a reflective person, an action taker, or both? To derive this information, interviewers may present to the candidate a hypothetical workplace problem and ask him or her to solve it.

Let's Play "Twenty Questions"

We have compiled the following list of questions based on our experience with personnel directors, executives in major corporations, and job placement firms (*aka* headhunters). Although this list is not exhaustive, it includes the questions most frequently asked at job interviews.

Question 1: *"What are your major strengths?"*

Suggestions: Polish your halo.

Select strengths that are related to high performance in the job for which you are applying. If, for instance, you are applying for a job as a stockbroker and your research, analytical, and interpersonal skills are strong, be sure to highlight them. When possible, offer examples that demonstrate you possess the characteristics you have mentioned.

If you do not believe that you have any strengths that are related to high job performance, you may be violating the goal satisfaction element in the Success Equation (see chapter 1). This job may not be for you.

Question 2: *"What are your major weaknesses?"*

Suggestions: The worst response is, "Honestly, I can't think of any."

Would *you* buy that answer to a question you'd asked?

Assuming that very few of us have achieved perfection, such an answer reveals arrogance, self-delusion, self-ignorance, intellectual apathy, or all four.

Nor do we recommend thinly veiling a strength as a weakness—"My biggest weakness is that I work too hard;" "My worst problem is that I am too thorough in my research." Such responses appear self-serving and phony.

Be honest and straightforward. Tell the interviewer what your greatest weakness is. He or she will probably find your candor refreshing.

The key in answering this question is what you say *after* you have revealed your weakness. Explain what steps or corrective action you have taken to resolve this weakness and the progress you have made. If, for instance, you're very shy, you may add that you are consciously trying to overcome this problem by speaking as much as possible in class, by making presentations before various groups, and by trying to meet people. Interviewers hire problem solvers, not people who run from problems...especially their own.

Question 3: *"What type of work experience can you bring to this job."*

Suggestions: Students are often concerned when interviewing that they have little job experience to describe. This should not be a major problem for you.

First, the interviewer *knows* that you are a student with limited workplace experience. Second, you can emphasize that the responsibilities you have successfully discharged in school are not unlike the responsibilities you will confront in the workplace. You have been given assignments as well as deadlines; you have had your work evaluated; you have worked in groups and independently; you have been asked to do both short-term and long-range projects; you have worked under stress; and you have learned to get along with some difficult people.

Even though you may never have had a full-time job, you are not without job-relevant experience!

Question 4: *"What do you see yourself doing five or ten years from now?"*

Suggestions: In order to focus your response, try to "read" what the interviewer is trying to evaluate.

Often the interviewer is trying to determine if you are committed to the firm. You may assure him or her that you do not intend to callously use this job for two or three years as a mere steppingstone to the job you really want. If, however, you are not sure how long you wish to stay with the firm, you may respond without committing yourself to a specific number of decades: "If the job remains interesting and the company and I are happy with each other, I could stay indefinitely."

Sometimes the interviewer is trying to determine if you have thought about what direction you would like your career to take. If this is the case, it is desirable to show that you have a career plan, but that you are flexible and open to new and unexpected opportunities.

Often the interviewer will be trying to assess both your commitment to the firm *and* your career plans with this question. You may wish, then, to include remarks on both of those issues in your response.

An excellent additional response (and, we hope, an honest one) to the question is to focus on learning: Talk about the skills and experience you hope to gain, the challenges you wish to confront, and the expertise you hope to achieve.

Question 5: *"Why do you want to work for us?"*

Suggestions: This question is a gift from the gods.

It allows you to show how your interests and abilities mesh with the job you are seeking. Delineate each of your talents, skills, and interests and demonstrate how each is related to the requirements of the job at hand. Your answer is the Success Equation come to life.

Furthermore, this question will allow you to show the interviewer that you have done some research on his or her company, which is not only flattering to the interviewer but also indicates that you are taking your application to this firm seriously:

Question 6: *"What do you think you can bring to this company?" Or "Why do you believe you are the right person for the job?"*

Suggestions: This question, which is habitually asked at job interviews, provides another wonderful opportunity for self-marketing.

Answering it effectively requires research *before* the interview. Find out what the company needs, what its managers are looking for, and then, based on your education, talents, and experience, demonstrate that you are a perfect fit for their opening.

Question 7: *"Discuss a project or undertaking in which you have been successful and explain why you believe you succeeded."*

Suggestions: If possible, discuss a project that you believe demanded similar abilities or experience as the job for which you are applying.

If, for instance, the prospective job requires the ability to work effectively as a part of a group, describe extracurricular activities, team sports, or community activities in which you have participated, enjoyed, and done well. If the prospective job demands the ability to manage people, discuss various leadership positions that you have held and the leadership style(s) you employed.

Question 8: *"Discuss something at which you did* not *succeed. What did you learn from the experience?"*

Suggestions: The key to answering this question is to explain what you have learned from the mistakes you have made and how that knowledge will help you on the job.

When describing your failure, avoid being defensive—if you have *not* failed at something, it is a sure sign that you have not done very much. Also avoid attributing failure to external factors—"It really wasn't my fault;" "The gods were against me;" "The ball took a bad bounce."

After taking your honest share of responsibility for the problem, discuss what steps you have taken to insure that a similar mistake will not occur in the future.

Question 9: *"How do you think your course work at school applies to this job?"*

Suggestions: Begin by describing how various courses gave you specific technical knowledge that will lead to job success.

This question may also be seen as an opportunity to discuss courses that have given you skills of a more general nature that will be needed on the job for which you are interviewing. If, for instance, the potential job requires interpersonal skills, you may wish to elucidate that aspect of your course work:

"My two-course sequence in human relations has helped me to become more empathetic as well as a better listener. I think these are important traits for someone working in customer relations."

Or: "Many of my courses required me to work in groups, and I think that experience will help me function as a member of the crisis intervention team."

Question 10: *"If you have supervised others, how do you think your staff would describe your management style?"*

Suggestions: If you have served as the president of a student group, the captain or co-captain of a team, or the chairperson of a project, describe the methods that you used to lead the group to achieve a specific goal.

You may also wish to discuss various problems that arose in working with this group and how you overcame them. Saying that you do not know how people felt about your leadership implies that you were not in touch with the group or simply didn't care about their feelings. If you have not held a leadership position, describe how you believe your classmates or coworkers saw you.

Question 11: *"What have you accomplished in the past that makes you think you can succeed in our company?"*

Suggestions: There are many tie-ins between the requirements for job success and your past accomplishments in school and elsewhere.

Success in the workplace, for instance, often means setting a goal and achieving it, characteristics common in becoming an Eagle Scout or class vice-president.

Success in the workplace often means possessing the ability to work with others, a skill you have learned while serving on various committees.

Success in the workplace often means the ability to budget your time, a skill you learned while simultaneously working at a part-time job, participating in extracurricular activities, and maintaining a solid grade point average.

A potential problem in responding to this question is that you may misdefine the meaning of "success in our company." If you do not know what "success" in this specific firm means, ask the interviewer to define it, or explain what you *believe* success means and ask for affirmation from the interviewer.

Question 12: *"How do you feel about working under stressful conditions?"*

Suggestions: If you abhor stressful tasks, then be honest with the interviewer and say so.

There is no point in getting a job that will wreak personal and emotional havoc on you. If you do not mind stress or thrive on the sense of excitement and challenge often associated with stress, let the interviewer see this quality in you.

You may also wish to describe how you deal with stress and maintain balance in your life: "I have learned to cope with stress in several ways. I find that jogging after school or work helps me to relax. I also block out one afternoon on the weekend for socializing and an evening for the movies."

Question 13: *"Would you describe yourself as a thinker or an action taker?"*

Suggestions: As with all questions, we recommend answering in a truthful, forthright fashion.

The problem with questions like this, however, is that they tend to label or pigeonhole a person. Even though the interviewer is asking a "black" or "white" question, there is no need to avoid a "gray" answer.

In reality, many of us are a combination of thinking and doing, and your response may suggest this: "In general, I would describe myself as a thinker. However, when a situation calls for action, I can act decisively. When I was chair of the dance committee, for instance, the band we hired cancelled two days before the dance. There was no time for discussion or hand wringing. I immediately telephoned other musical groups and booked a replacement the same afternoon."

Question 14: *"Describe a goal you have set for yourself in the past and how you went about attaining it."*

Suggestions: The interviewer may have several reasons for asking you this.

He or she may want to know if you are goal directed, if your actions are based on a carefully planned strategy or intuition, if you are tenacious in attaining your goals, and if you are creative in overcoming obstacles in the pursuit of a goal. If you cannot readily think of examples, think of "goals" in broad terms—trying to show an instructor that you could do well in his or her class, demonstrating to yourself that you could learn a foreign language, or wanting to show a summer employer that you could sell effectively are all goals.

In answering this question, walk the interviewer through the steps you took to achieve your objective. Discuss the external problems you faced (lack of time, physical difficulties, inadequate funding) as well as the internal problems (frustration, self-doubt, anxiety). Then focus on how you coped with or overcame these obstacles.

Question 15: *"Pick someone in the business or professional world you admire and explain why you respect this individual."*

Suggestions: The interviewer is probably trying to identify your role models so that he or she can extrapolate the characteristics you most admire.

Your answer should go well beyond simply naming a famous individual and saying that you wish to be like that person because he or she is successful. What are the characteristics, values, beliefs, and methods of working with others that went into that person's success? What personal characteristics do you respect?

You may also discuss your admiration of someone from the recent past—Martin Luther King, John F. Kennedy, Albert Schweitzer—whose beliefs, goals, or accomplishments you admire.

Question 16: *"What do you do for fun? What are your personal interests?"*

Suggestions: This question allows you to present yourself as a three-dimensional person...

...one who enjoys music, likes to travel, plays sports, and collects rare coins. Take advantage of any personal interest that would suggest a good fit between you and your potential job or you and the organization. Many companies put a premium on community service. If you have had community involvement, be sure to mention it.

Question 17: *"I note from your resume that: a) you have a three-year gap in your work history; b) you have held six jobs over the last three years; c) you have no experience in one area crucial to success in this job; or d) you have not listed your grade point average. Please explain."*

Suggestions: Most interviewers will identify a weakness or potential problem in your background, experience, or education. Anticipate your Achilles' heel and prepare a response.

Be honest. If you do not have a high grade point average, admit this, but offer to explain why it is not better. Perhaps you worked 20 hours a week to pay for personal expenses. Perhaps you lacked motivation when you started school and thus failed to study during your freshman and sophomore years. You then saw the importance of education and became more committed to academics. In this case, you should point to your current grade point average as evidence.

There may, however, be a skeleton in your closet that you cannot facilely explain. In this case, you need to convince the interviewer that you are aware of the problem, have dealt with it (or are currently dealing with it successfully), and believe that it will not affect your job performance.

You may also turn a deficiency into a potential benefit: "You're correct in noting that I have jumped from job to job over the past three years. The problem was that I had no focus on what kind of work I wanted to do. I was searching. I think that time is behind me now. I have given a lot of thought to working in law enforcement. In fact, I have learned from my past experience that I take great pleasure and pride in helping people."

Question 18: *"Are you married? Are you pregnant? Does your spouse work? Are you divorced? Are you planning to have a family? How many children do you have?"*

Suggestions: If these questions are not directly job-related, they may be considered unlawful to ask under state, federal, and/or local law.

Although these questions are generally *not* job-related and asking them *may* be unlawful, some interviewers will not let that deter them from poking into your personal life.

Whether you choose to answer such questions is your decision. The issue should be resolved in your own mind, however, and a decision made *before* you attend an interview. If you do not have serious moral or ethical qualms about answering such questions, we recommend that you respond to them. If you *do*, however, express your point of view in a diplomatic and tactful fashion: "I don't mean to be difficult, but I know that legally I am not obliged to answer questions about my religion for a job of this nature. I'm sure you have your reasons for asking the question and I respect that, but I would prefer to go on to other questions."

One caveat: Answering the question in this manner could decrease your chances of getting the job. But then, the workplace is not always fair or rational.

Question 19: *"Did you finance your education yourself, or did you receive assistance from your family?"*

Suggestions: The answer to this question may help the interviewer place some deficiencies in your resume in the proper context.

A less-than-spectacular grade point average or a spotty record of extracurricular activities could be explained by the fact that you provided total or substantial support for yourself during school. While interviewers will probably be impressed by students who worked their way through school, having received financial support from your family will not necessarily place you at a disadvantage.

Question 20: *"Describe the type of supervisor or manager for whom you would like to work."*

Suggestions: Tell the interviewer the type of person for whom you would ideally like to work; e.g., a "hands-on" boss, an autocrat, one who gives you autonomy, one who holds a tight reign.

Explain why you think certain leadership styles are preferable to others. Stress, however—if it is true—that you are flexible, ready and able to adapt to various managerial styles.

There is your 20-question exam. How are you going to prepare for the time when you have to deal with it face-to-face?

First, write down your answers to each question. Mulling over some general responses in your mind is not sufficient. Writing is a form of thinking. You will not see problems in your responses, gaps in your logic, or holes in your arguments *until* you commit your answers to paper.

Give yourself several hours, over a weekend or even a few days, to write responses to these questions. At the end of each response, add a one-sentence answer to the following question: "What are the one or two key points I just made?"

Highlight these so that you can use them as a quick "study guide" before an interview.

The next step is to role-play an interview with another person. Doing so will help you make the transition from written responses to an interactive, face-to-face verbal exchange. Ask for hard-nosed, gloves-off feedback. Knee-jerk defensive reactions should be avoided, since it is better to hear the bad news now rather than later.

Videotaping equipment is readily available at most high schools, colleges, and universities—you may want to film your interview and review your performance.

The Style And Tone Of An Effective Interview

Be seen as a problem solver, as an individual who can find practical, thoughtful, and creative ways of dealing with job-related difficulties. Employers benefit from—and thus are inclined to *hire*—individuals who look at problems as challenges and not obstacles, who dwell on solutions rather than all the reasons why solutions won't work. It is much better to say, "There are three ways I would approach that problem," than, "I'm glad that I don't have to clean up *that* mess!"

Be positive in the tone and content of your responses. If you bad-mouth people, always pointing an accusing finger and blaming *others'* mistakes or stupidity, you will generally succeed only in creating a negative and unprofessional image of *yourself.*

Maximize options. Avoid saying, "I'm really not interested in working in that part of your company," or "I really don't want a job in sales, as I think you're suggesting." At this point you probably don't have enough specific information about the job or company to be able to make an informed assessment. Do not prematurely rule out *any* possibilities or options. If you decide that specific aspects of a job are not acceptable to you after obtaining additional information and reflecting upon the issue, this should be expressed and re-solved after the job has been *offered*, but before you have accepted it.

Market yourself with taste. Self-confidence should never become egocentricity or vanity. Overselling yourself, even in jest—"How would you like to hire the greatest miracle worker since Moses?"—will often be perceived as an attempt to hide feelings of insecurity and inadequacy.

Create an impression of personal enthusiasm and energy. Demonstrate excitement for your past accomplishments and spirited optimism over your future goals. Vocal inflections, expressive use of your hands, and maintaining eye contact will help an interviewer feel your energy.

Never leave a negative hanging out on a limb. Show the interviewer that you recognize the weaknesses in your back-ground and are striving to overcome them.

If, for instance, an interviewer asks, "How can someone as smart as you receive grades of 'D,' 'E,' and 'D' in two basic science courses and one accounting course?" you may wish to respond, "To be honest, I got what I deserved. I received those grades during my sophomore year, when I was studying parties more than books. When I realized the foolishness and immaturity of what I was doing, I turned things around. You'll note that my grades improved greatly in the semesters that followed. I learned a lot from that experience that will benefit me in the future: If you are going to do something well, you had better commit yourself to it rather than trying to do a half-baked job."

Express balanced views and perspectives. This does not mean that you have to appear as a wishy-washy blob of proto-plasm or a "mugwump" (people who have their *mug* on one side of the fence and their *wump* on the other). It *does* mean, however, that you have the maturity and intelligence to see issues in their true complexities, that you have the ability to penetrate beneath the deceptively simple-looking veneer of a problem. Extremism, dogmatism, inflexibility, or self-right-eousness are out of place at an interview.

Avoid distasteful remarks. Avoid remarks or jokes that may in any way be interpreted as sexist, racist, or ethnically offensive—no matter how funny you think they are. Assume a high level of sensitivity on the part of the interviewer and in the business world in general.

When appropriate, give answers with depth and examples. Do not simply say *what* you did; explain *why* you did it. Doing so will add strength and completeness to your answers. It will allow the interviewer to see your perceptiveness and awareness, the depth of your understanding, and your mind at work.

Examples are a valuable means of illustrating our thoughts. They will help the interviewer to understand you better and to remember your responses.

Be yourself. Polonius's advice to his son in "Hamlet" is as relevant today as it was almost four centuries ago:

This above all, to thine own self be true,
And it must follow as the night the day
Thou canst not then be false to any man.

Relax and allow your true personality to emerge. Let the interviewer see in a natural and unforced way the traits that have endeared you to your friends—sincerity, warmth, commitment, sensitivity, kindness. A sense of self-irony, the ability to laugh at yourself and the mistakes you have made, will not only impress an interviewer but also help you achieve a successful career. Pretentiousness, phony facades, inappropriate name-dropping, and supercilious poses are anathema, in both interviews and life.

Ethics in Terra Incognita

Do you tell the truth in job interviews? The answer should be "Yes," but the issue can get cloudy. Consider the following three scenarios.

Scenario 1: You have applied for a job as an airplane mechanic. You are qualified for the job except for one item: You have no sensation in two of your fingers, the result of a childhood injury. There is a substantial likelihood that the loss of feeling in those fingers will impede your job performance. Should you mention this physical problem at the job interview?

Scenario 2: You were elected captain of the girls' basketball team at your school in your junior year, but your teammates disliked your dogmatic leadership style and did not re-elect you in your senior year. If the interviewer asks why you were not re-elected, how should you respond?

Scenario 3: You suffered from emotional and psychological problems several years ago, but you have recovered from them. Do you divulge this information to the interviewer?

These questions, and many others like them, may seem difficult to answer. You may not be sure what to do. Our advice is very simple—**Always tell the truth**. End of confusion.

Lying or misrepresentation is morally and ethically wrong. Your potential employer has the right to know if there are any aspects of your education, personality, background, personal and professional experience, or physical capabilities that may put him or his clients at risk. Furthermore, if it becomes known that you lied or misrepresented yourself at the job interview, your employment could be terminated.

Candor and truthfulness, of course, is a two-way street. Your potential employer must give *you* a realistic description of the job for which you are applying, including information about risks, hazards, stress, and any unusual demands that are intrinsic to it.

A job interview is an ideal time for your potential employer to determine if you are right for the job and for you to determine if the job is right for you. Without candor and truthfulness on both sides, neither of you will be able to make an informed decision.

In the first scenario, we think that you are ethically required to tell your interviewer that you have a physical disability that could hamper your job performance. Once this has been revealed, you and the interviewer can discuss manual tasks that you can perform effectively, job areas where your condition would not be disabling, and various accommodations that could be made for your disability.

In the second scenario, this issue need not be raised by you. If, however, you are specifically asked why you were not re-elected, you are pretty much obligated to state that a majority of the members of the team disliked your leadership style and, thus, did not vote for you (you need *not* mention that they starting calling you "Commandante").

This experience, however, should be put in a larger context. You may explain why you adopted a specific type of leadership style. If you believe your judgment was poor, you may wish to discuss what you have learned from the experience and how you have changed your leadership techniques. You may also wish to mention the successes you have had in leading other groups.

In the third scenario, be fair to yourself and your potential employer. If your emotional or psychological problems have been resolved or are currently being properly managed, you need not mention those problems, even if asked. If, however, there is still a question about how well they are being managed, you should explain those problems to the interviewer. You should, of course, also explain the efforts you are making to deal with them.

Should you mention emotional, psychological, or other problems if the interviewer does not specifically ask about them? Truthfulness sometimes necessitates that you take the initiative in making disclosures. If you have a problem or condition that will adversely affect your potential employer or his clients, you must discuss this issue with the interviewer.

Even though you may not have disabilities or conditions that would seriously affect your ability to discharge job responsibilities, it is not uncommon to be asked a question that may reveal something negative about yourself. Be truthful, but, when possible, provide a context for your answer that will still give you the best possible chance to get the job.

Little Things Mean A Lot

The words to the Joni James song apply to interviews as well as to love. Here are some "little things" we recommend:

- Expect the interviewer to be unprepared. Bring extra copies of your resume, and be prepared to help the interviewer do some basic learning about you. Do not get angry, even if the interviewer's conduct is rude.

- Dress slightly more conservatively than the manner in which company employees generally dress.

- Get to the interview about ten minutes early. Arriving late obviously creates a negative impression.

- Be professional and pleasant to secretaries. The interview may go well, but if secretaries tell the interviewer you were rude or displayed a condescending attitude, it may undermine your efforts.

- Do not ask about salary or fringe benefits. Allow the interviewer to bring these up. If these issues are not raised, fear not. If you are offered the job (or are called back for another interview), they will be discussed soon enough. If the interviewer asks what your salary requirements are, give a *range* that may be modified by the type of fringe benefit programs the firm offers. Be sure to mention that you are more interested in the content of the job—its responsibilities, challenges, and career development potential—than simply in salary, and that these elements will play the greatest part in your final decision.

- Ask about the next step: When will you be notified about subsequent interviews, job testing, or a final decision? Not only will this help you deal with personal anxiety, but it will also show your prospective employer that you are a serious candidate.

- Send a thank-you note. If you interviewed with five people, send *five* separate notes, specifically tailored to the people with whom you spoke.

Asking *Your* Questions

Interviews are two-way streets. While an interviewer is judging you, you are simultaneously judging the interviewer and the firm he or she represents. Toward the conclusion of most interviews, you will be asked if you have any questions about the firm or the nature of the work. This is an appropriate time to raise issues that have been on your mind. Remember, a good job is one which is **mutually beneficial**: The employee contributes to the welfare of the firm, and the firm contributes to the welfare, growth, and development of the employee.

To devise intelligent questions, learn as much as you can about the firm, its products and services, and the job for which you are applying before the interview. Read annual reports, consult *Barrons*, look up articles in news magazines such as *Forbes, Business Week,* and *U.S. News and World Report*. Call the company and ask to be sent material describing its history and current status. Talk to anyone who works for the company or in a related field. Placement offices at many high schools and colleges maintain files of alumni employed by major corporations who are willing to discuss their work with job candidates. Information from such sources will help you make a forceful, positive impression.

Asking perceptive, probing questions is also a good interviewing strategy. Questions such as, "I noted in your annual report that you are moving more and more into consumer products and away from heavy industry. Has this strategy been successful?" shows the interviewer that you have done your homework. It is perfectly permissible to write down questions and consult your notes during the interview.

Most of all, get used to and try to enjoy the process. It may be your *first* interview. It is most assuredly not your *last*.

Four

LIVING IN UNCHARTED LANDS: THE JOB OFFER AND DECISION

It may take a while. It may even seem like an eternity. But your campus to corporation transition *will* proceed and a job offer *will* be made. Your first reaction will be to do a double backward flip that would make an Olympic gymnast proud. You will be overcome with joy because someone values you and actually wants you!

Although it may take every scintilla of self-restraint that you can muster, *do not immediately accept the offer,* even if you are certain that the job is tailor made for you. Intense gratitude is not the stuff of intelligent decisions.

Buy Time

When your potential employer calls you (offers are generally made on the phone or in follow-up meetings; rejections are sent through the mail), you may certainly tell him or her how thrilled you are, but *ask for at least one week to decide.* If he or she can only grant you two or three days, that will have to do. (It is unlikely for him or her to demand a decision in three minutes.) The following are fairly typical ways to buy time so that you can think about your decision:

"I'm thrilled about the job offer. I hope you don't mind, but I know from experience that it's best for me to sit down for a week to give important decisions like this more thought. May I call you back next Monday with my answer?

"In the meantime, would you please send me a letter confirming your offer and the terms of my employment? If there is an employment contract, would you send that along as well?"

Or: "I'm delighted about the job offer. There are a few people I would like to speak to before I formally accept the offer, so I would appreciate it if I could have about a week before I get back to you. In the meantime, would you please send me a letter which confirms your offer and the terms of my employment? If there is an employment contract, would you send that along as well?"

And *do* request a formal *letter of offer*. The letter should include your starting salary, job responsibilities, description of benefits, and any other details of your proposed employment. This will give you a record of precisely what you have been offered so that misunderstandings or miscommunications will be minimized.

If you are asked to sign an employment contract, read it carefully, and have an attorney review it with you.

Rethink...Everything

Although no guarantee of infallibility, *informed* decisions—those based on factual information rationally analyzed—are generally *sound* decisions. It is now time to gather even more data about the firm and the nature of your job.

Organize any notes you made before the interview. Commit to paper your reflections on the interview itself. Be sure you know your specific job responsibilities, including to whom you report. If you have questions, do not hesitate to call or visit your interviewer. Talk to individuals who may be familiar with the company or your type of job and pick their brains for whatever information they can offer.

Focus On Content, Not Candy

Be sure to focus on the *content* of the job offer, not on the sugar-coated wooing or ego-boosting overtures of your potential employer. Although "sweet-recruiting nothings" often make an objective decision difficult, it is vital to examine and respond to the substance and content of the offer, especially to your job responsibilities and the potential for personal and professional growth. While reviewing all aspects of the job offer, prioritize those elements that are especially important to you and determine if the job offer meets your expectations.

Salary Considerations

If the salary you are offered is slightly lower than you had expected, don't haggle over a small sum of money at the risk of losing the future good will of your employer. If you wish to determine if the salary offered is appropriate, find out what average salaries for entry-level positions in your field, in your geographical region, and for people with your experience and education are. Factor into your salary all fringe benefits that are included with the job.

If your research suggests that you are being *substantially* underpaid, diplomatically explain this to your prospective employer and ask him or her to review the situation. Demonstrate your willingness to compromise. If, for instance, your prospective employer cannot increase your salary significantly, you may be able to negotiate for payment of moving expenses, travel costs, or an increase in any year-end bonuses.

If your negotiations prove futile but you still like the job, the Success Equation suggests that you should accept the offer. While you certainly deserve to get paid what you are worth, task interest and goal satisfaction are the most important considerations at this point. If you are interested in what you are doing, you will do a better job. The better job you do, the more you will eventually make.

What About Pending Offers?

While going through this sometimes agonizing process, you may be waiting to hear from other prospective employers, hoping that they will call before your decision must be made. The ball is not entirely in their court. Speak to employers where your application is pending, letting them know that, although you have received an offer, you are still interested in their firm and would like to know the status of your application.

Decision Time

If, after amassing and analyzing as much relevant data as you can, you have serious reservations about the firm or the nature of the job you will be doing, *turn the offer down.* You want a job, as we suggested in the Success Equation, that excites and challenges you and allows you to achieve satisfying goals. As important as salary may seem at this stage of your life, you should be reasonably selective in your first transition and wait for a job that fulfills most of your expectations.

Agonizing over a job decision is not unusual; in fact, it would be somewhat surprising if you did not have conflicting emotions, internal turmoil, sweaty palms, and a nervous stomach. The anxieties you are experiencing are perfectly human; since they generally serve to protect your self-interests, they are even beneficial.

One way to manage the dissonance is to review the various "Interest Themes" you delineated in chapter 1 and examine your job offer in light of them. If possible, discuss your evaluation with family, friends, and career advisers at school. After gathering data, talking to people, and analyzing the information you have collected, a decision must be made. It is your decision—it must be based on what you think is best for you.

In addition to rational analysis, we also believe in the value and trustworthiness of intuition. If a job or a firm "feels" right to you, that should be given high priority in your evaluation.

Accepting A Job

Although you may accept a job offer verbally, send a written acceptance to your new employer. Do not make any unsolicited commitments in your letter of acceptance (e.g., "I am willing to commit myself for the next five years to your company"). After the firm has received your letter of acceptance and has again confirmed the job offer (you should have received by now a formal, written job offer), and *only at this point,* write to the organizations with whom your application is still pending, notifying them that you have accepted a different offer.

Mistakes At The Job-Offer Stage

Here are some of the more common mistakes individuals make at this important stage of their first career transition:

- *Formally accepting a job offer and then rescinding it because you receive a better offer a few days later.* At best, your original employer will perceive this as an immature act; at worst, it will be seen as unprofessional and unethical conduct. Earning this type of reputation, as well as burning your bridges, may undermine your career in the future. Be sure the job is what you want *before* accepting it.

- *Accepting a job offer but leaving your applications pending elsewhere.* This generally occurs as a result of idle curiosity ("Could I have gotten that other job?") or a lack of commitment to your present employer. This practice is unfair to the firms at which your application is still alive, to individuals competing for the same jobs, to your present employer, and to yourself. It reduces your ability to make a psychological commitment to your new position and your new responsibilities. When you accept a job offer, make a clean break from other alternatives by writing a polite and appreciative letter withdrawing your application.

- *Forgetting the people who helped you at each stage in obtaining your job.* Write thank-you notes to all your references and to those special individuals who held your hand and offered you advice and counsel. It is thoughtful, as well as prudent, if you want to build a network of people who can assist you in the future.

- *Comparing your job offer to those of your friends.* Such comparisons are pointless; it is only important that *you* are pleased with your job offer. The best comparisons you can make throughout your career are with yourself—e.g., "Have I grown professionally during the past year?" "Am I better off today than I was a year ago?"

Events are transpiring in your life at a dizzying place. You have, in a few short months, gone from perhaps only a vague idea of what you wanted to do for a living to having selected and secured a job which should bring you personal and professional satisfaction.

The toboggan ride is not over, however. You have now entered the shifting and changing world of the workplace.

Hang on. The ride is just beginning.

Five

Strategies For Success: The First Year

It has been described variously as a "rude awakening," "growing up," or "entering the real world." Regardless of the epithets, beginning employment at a new firm constitutes a major change in your life. One of the best techniques for minimizing the problems and maximizing the opportunities in any career transition is precise and astute planning. We hope the following suggestions, while they may appear avuncular, will assist you during your period of orientation.

Work Starts Before *You* Start Work

Immediately after your employer receives your letter of acceptance, call or visit your new boss and ask him or her to supply you with reading materials pertinent to your work. These may differ substantially from the documents that you used to prepare for your job interview. Sales reports, organizational charts, profit and loss statements, project assignments, account histories, technical information on company products, and the company handbook on policies and procedures will provide you with a much-needed context for understanding and discharging your new responsibilities.

If possible, ask your boss to suggest a coworker with whom you may meet to discuss nuts-and-bolts matters before your job begins. The first week on a new job is filled with so many distractions that absorbing work-related information at that time is extremely difficult.

What kinds of distractions? You name them and they are present:

Learning peoples' names, finding a parking space, registering pertinent information in the company's personnel system,

MEETINGS,

Finding a stapler, figuring out where to go for lunch, getting your typewriter fixed,

MEETINGS,

Introducing yourself to colleagues, wondering what your boss is really like, wondering what your boss's boss is really like,

MEETINGS,

Wondering if your coworkers will accept you, figuring out what and how much work to take home, and, of course,

MEETINGS.

Day One is anxiety day. It is also the day that you will be convinced that "Murphy's Law" ("If anything can go wrong, it will") and its legion of corrolaries were written expressly with you in mind.

Learn Names

As soon as you are alone, write down the names and job titles of the people you meet. Addressing people by their names when you see them for the second time will please your colleagues and help you experience a sense of belonging.

Listen for how people address one another. Do coworkers, for instance, refer to each other by their first names? Are bosses addressed by "Mr.," "Mrs.," or "Ms."? When are titles used?

Learn The Culture Of The Firm

Companies, like people, have unique and distinctive personalities. Yours will have a certain value system, modes of acceptable and unacceptable behavior, systems of rewards and punishments, likes and dislikes, sacred cows and closet skeletons. The culture and personality of a firm must be understood before it is to be engaged or challenged.

We know of an unfortunate case: Thomas J., a recent law school graduate, had not bothered to familiarize himself with his firm's sacred heritage. Hanging on the walls of the reception area were portraits of the firm's founding fathers, most of whom looked like the faces on a box of Smith Brothers cough drops.

On his way to lunch with a senior partner, he pointed to one of the portraits and quipped, "Now there is one unfriendly looking man." The senior partner, inhaling deeply, barked back, "My grandfather, that unfriendly looking man, is the reason you currently have a job."

Foot-in-mouth disease is to be studiously avoided, especially with upper management.

Firms, like people, also have a negative side to their personalities. You will soon learn—whether you want to or not—about office romances, incompetent secretaries, boardroom backstabbings, office politics, and your boss's secret desire to build a sales pyramid in China. This "other," shadowy organization will slowly unfold before your eyes and ears. Allow this information to come to you; learn without getting personally involved. (You may wish to regard such information with a healthy skepticism.) By maintaining your distance from this darker side of the workplace, you will also maintain your credibility, integrity, and job security.

The culture and personality of a firm are revealed in seemingly endless ways. Bulletin board announcements of training seminars may indicate a corporate culture that values education and staying on the cutting edge. Notices about social events or team sports may suggest that participation in group activities and socializing outside of work are the norm—perhaps even expected.

The size and location of offices may tell you something about priorities within an organization. Do people in sales have larger offices in a more central locale than those in operations? If so, what does this suggest to you about how resources are allocated within the firm?

Sparsely decorated offices and corridors may suggest a frugal, no-nonsense corporate philosophy. An abundance of pictures and wall decorations and plush furniture may denote a firm that values warmth, conviviality, and symbols of success. Desks in offices placed between the visitor and the employee may suggest a degree of formality and conservatism that one would not sense in offices in which desks are placed against the walls, thereby removing any physical barrier between the visitor and the employee.

Reading the culture and personality of a firm, learning what a company values and abhors, is crucial to your success. Doing so will increase your sensitivity to and understanding of why people and organizations act in certain ways. But don't jump to conclusions based on limited information. A good researcher evaluates data carefully, collects information from a variety of sources, and constantly tests his or her conclusions against alternative explanations.

Proceed Cautiously

Don't expect to hit a home run during your first few weeks. Keep your eyes and ears open, ask questions selectively, and be a good listener. Naturally, you should be courteous and amiable, but do not feel compelled to form intimate friendships or have intense heart-to-hearts after your first meeting with a person.

Insecurity and anxiety often cause us to come on too strongly, to unburden our souls and reveal our innermost thoughts and fears to even casual acquaintances. People often react negatively to this type of behavior and may immediately regard this obtrusive newcomer with suspicion.

A coworker who knows about your intimate problems may feel that if you would blab about yourself, you also would talk about the secrets of others.

A boss conversant with your personal problems and limitations, while sympathetic, may be reluctant to give you additional responsibilities...and the promotions that go with them.

Getting Along With Your Boss

Bosses like resourceful employees with a positive attitude. They like people who, when a difficult task needs to be done, will immediately declare, "Why not *me?*" instead of "Why me?" They like people who are willing to help the firm in ways not included in their job descriptions, people who are willing to stay until midnight, if necessary, to complete an assignment. Negative-thinking, clock-watching employees are ignored; resourceful, self-motivated, and positive employees are promoted.

Learn to "read" what your boss wants. Does he or she like short or long explanations? Does he or she want to hear about all the problems in a unit or only the major ones? Does he or she make a fetish out of punctuality and deadlines? How well informed about a project does he or she wish to be? Is he or she more approachable in the morning or the afternoon?

Learning a boss's modus operandi and idiosyncrasies will help you become a more effective and valued employee.

This Isn't Kansas, Toto

Since you just left school, it's important you quickly come to understand some of the basic differences between an academic environment and the workplace.

Tasks in an academic environment tend to be reasonably well-defined: You know the assignments for which you are responsible and when the work must be completed.

Assignments and deadlines in the workplace are generally not as precisely delineated. You will often be expected to set your own deadlines, make critical decisions on how to allocate your time and energies, decide when a task has been completed, and determine when and how a completed task should be evaluated.

Our recommendation: Commit to paper your weekly goals and responsibilities, discuss these matters with your boss, and prioritize your time in terms of the demands that are being made on you.

Evaluation of performance and when such evaluations will occur are generally clearly enunciated in the academic world. Every quarter or semester your grade point average tells you exactly, to the hundredth place, where you stand.

This is more the exception than the rule in the workplace. While formal performance appraisals do exist, they are often misapplied, misunderstood, begrudgingly conducted, or, with surprising frequency, not conducted at all.

It is imperative, however, that you get frequent feedback on your performance. If it is not supplied by your immediate superior or your colleagues, request it.

There is little point to working in a self-deluded world; honest appraisal and constructive suggestions are vital to a successful career.

Hold Thy Tongue

The desideratum in <u>The Book Of Common Prayer</u> to keep "my tongue from evil-speaking...and slandering" is especially applicable to the workplace. In college you could "let it all hang out" and vociferously criticize professors and administrators with impunity. In the workplace, bad mouthing a superior is likely to bring your career to a crashing halt. Gossiping about a peer is just as bad.

Money, Money Everywhere!

Your lifestyle will change dramatically when you change from student to employee. One of the first changes is that you will begin to spend money as though you were printing it on your private press. Now that you have a steady income, you will be less reluctant to make substantial purchases on credit. As any Keynesian will tell you, saving money at a bank instead of spending it undermines the national economy. (It is curious how many people become card-carrying Keynesians shortly after the transition to their first job.) The key to financial security is planning, and again, it begins *before* you start your first job.

Maintaining a cash flow is critical, especially if you are moving to another city. Construct a budget that both prioritizes your expenses and ensures ready cash. At the same time, consider debt reduction as an investment. Although you will be establishing a household, it is not necessary to purchase everything you desire at once. Avoid big-ticket items, especially a car, until you can absorb the expense. Consider renting items such as a television or a stereo system until you can afford to buy them.

Although we live in a society of instant gratification, in which postponing purchases seems almost un-American, career transitions often limit one's financial options, and there is no time like the present to become accustomed to that notion.

The 6th Day Of The Workweek

Saturday will become more important to you than it has ever been in the past. It is the day on which you will do most of the personal chores and attend to many of the private needs that you had previously stretched out over an entire week.

You will quickly find that numerous professional services (e.g., medical, dental, banking, investment services) are offered on Saturday precisely for people like you.

At the risk of sounding trendy, let us recommend one popular piece of technology that will help you make the transition in your personal life from student to professional. If you are addicted, as many students are, to watching late-night T.V. and find it difficult to break the habit, buy or rent a video cassette recorder. It will allow you to tape the shows and movies you want and watch them when time permits—often on Saturday.

Have Realistic Expectations

You may become resentful of your job soon after the excitement of having one wears off. This is not an unusual development. After all, this new job has radically altered your comfortable lifestyle. It has deprived you of much of your private time and left you with less control over your schedule and, ultimately, yourself than at any time since you were a child.

When looking at your superiors, you may well become convinced that you are seeing the "Peter Principle" in action—"In a hierarchy every employee tends to rise to the level of his or her incompetence."

While you may be convinced that you are not being appreciated rapidly enough, you may also be pulled in the opposite direction, suffering from poignant pangs of insecurity and self-doubt reminiscent, perhaps, of when you were entering puberty.

While there are no easy solutions to this problem—just as there were no easy solutions to puberty—anticipating these feelings and realizing that your fears and doubts and resentments are shared by others making a similar transition may help you to adjust to your new role.

Have realistic expectations of your job, your future, and yourself during this demanding period. As a "junior person" you may well receive the worst assignments, have the credit for your achievements usurped by ambitious superiors, and be required to work long hours. All for relatively little pay. You may find that no matter how much you accomplish, it is never quite enough. If you have the distinct impression that you are serving an apprenticeship, it is an impression based on truth.

Virtually all professionals serve an apprenticeship, and this should not be viewed as demeaning or unfair. Your apprenticeship is a time of rapid growth and development, and it is the foundation upon which you will build a successful career.

It All Adds Up

While you are probably feeling a great deal of pressure and confusion from starting a new job and may occasionally feel "down," focus on the many positive events that are occurring in your professional life.

In a brief period of time, you've learned new skills, discovered and developed hidden talents, formed new friendships, and begun a life as an independent, self-supporting individual.

Mr. Chips would be proud.

Six

STRATEGIES FOR SUCCESS: THE NEXT NINE YEARS

Now that you have successfully navigated through the potholes and speed traps of the first few months, we hope that your heart and breathing rates have returned to normal. You have recently begun a long career journey that will take you through a lifetime of experiences and challenges, brainstorms and thunderstorms, gentle breezes and roaring gales. We offer in this chapter some recommendations that will hopefully keep you roaring down the expressway and away from the detours.

Remember: You Are There To Learn And Work

This lesson is as important as it is obvious. It is all too easy to spend hours at work in activities not directly related to learning and performing your job—pouring over your benefit package, idly chatting with your colleagues, reading the newspaper, planning your weekend.

While no one will begrudge you an occasional break, your time and energy at work should be devoted to learning your job from top to bottom, side to side, and front to back, and then doing it as well as you possibly can. All other activities at work, while not entirely without value, should be subordinated to the bedrock of a successful career: learning and doing.

Support Your Boss

We discussed in the last chapter the importance of getting along with your boss. Supporting your boss is equally as vital to your job success. Here are several ways you can be a supportive employee:

Initiate. Be proactive rather than reactive. Anticipate assignments that have to be done and offer to do them instead of waiting for them to be placed in your lap. If a particularly difficult task must be undertaken, let it be known that you are prepared and willing to do it.

Disagree when necessary. If, after thorough analysis, you believe your boss is wrong, discuss the reasons for your disagreement with him or her. Expressing your reservations over an issue should be done in private and in a diplomatic, non-combative fashion. You may wish to begin such an exchange with a question like, "May we look one last time at our marketing campaign?" And, if the decision goes against you...

Put it behind you. Support your boss even if he or she does not follow your recommendations. Honest disagreements or differences of opinion occur often, and you should not feel personally rebuked or embarrassed if your boss disagrees with you. What is important is that you have expressed an idea and that it has been fairly and objectively considered.

Know your audience. One of the best ways to support a boss is to be sensitive to his or her personality traits. We talked to an employee in a marketing research company, for example, who said that his boss was extremely intense and anxious. If the boss thought that a survey had been lost, he would become an emotional wreck.

To be supportive, this employee never uttered a word about a misplaced survey or one that could not be instantly found.

Only when he was absolutely sure that a survey was lost did he report this fact to his boss.

Be dependable. Send the message to your boss that he or she can always count on you. Being punctual, meeting (or beating) deadlines, offering to help in a squeeze, volunteering for a difficult job will let your boss know that you are a loyal, reliable, and supportive employee.

Learn to Manage a Difficult Boss

Although you may be working at a *job* that you enjoy, you may find that you do *not* enjoy your *boss*. The first step in establishing a congenial working relationship with him or her is to determine who is at fault. Yes, it *may* be you: If you are especially sensitive to criticism, then you would probably react negatively to *any* boss who liked to offer suggestions for improvement. If you cherish autonomy, you would probably chafe at the bit with *any* boss who employed a highly directive leadership style.

If, after being brutally honest with yourself, you conclude that the fault lies with you and not with your boss, then it is up to you to modify your attitudes, behavior, and reactions in order to get along with him or her.

When an individual cannot get along with a boss, it is often because the relationship is not fulfilling the needs of one or both parties. Employees are well aware of their own needs: to be treated fairly; understand what is expected of them; given an opportunity to succeed; establish a support network; receive feedback, approval and recognition for a job well done; and to be challenged, respected, and liked.

What may *not* be as obvious, however, is that bosses have similar needs. A productive, congenial relationship between a boss and a subordinate is based largely on recognizing each other's needs and fulfilling them. If your boss is not meeting your needs, ideally you should discuss the matter with him or her. This, of course, assumes that you have an open and honest relationship with your boss. If this is not the case, then other remedies must be sought.

You may wish to use rewards to influence your boss's behavior toward you. If, for instance, you would like he or she to give you more autonomy, express your gratitude when you are given the barest smidgen of independence. If you desire more direction and guidance from your boss, be sure to remark on how helpful you have found his or her advice. Remember, bosses also want to be liked and appreciated; a positive reaction from you should encourage similar behavior in the future.

If this does not work, you may want to find a substitute to fulfill your needs. If, for example, your boss does not give you sufficient feedback on your work, you may wish to discuss your activities with another manager or your coworkers and ask them for feedback.

Since your boss may be piqued that you are requesting guidance elsewhere, ask these individuals to keep their counseling confidential. Creating this type of support system may not change your boss, but it will allow you to overcome the difficulty of working for someone who is not meeting one of your important needs.

Being able to "read" your boss will also help you avoid problems. If your boss is under a great deal of stress, a measure of impatience, curtness, or even rudeness should be taken with a grain of salt.

Learn when to stay clear and when to approach, when to disagree and when to remain silent, when to offer help and when to stay on the sidelines.

If all your attempts to establish a congenial working relationship with your boss have proved futile, then, and *only* then, should you contemplate transferring to another department or leaving the firm. The latter action, of course, should not be done rashly, for it represents not a solution to the problem but the failure of solutions.

And always remember one important fact: The workplace is *not* always fair. As a younger employee, you must be prepared to compromise more than you would like, to meet a boss more than half way, to bite your tongue until you feel it swelling. If you are flexible and have kept the lines of communication open, two rational people should be able, more often than not, to resolve the problems that have arisen between them.

Support Your Coworkers

You not only work *for* someone, you also work *with* others. Professional success and personal well-being involve your relationship with your coworkers as well as your boss. How well you accomplish your assignments will often depend on the degree of support you receive from your coworkers, while their friendship is a valuable ingredient in your social support network.

The recommendations we have made for how to be a supportive subordinate apply equally well to being a supportive coworker. If your colleagues are floundering, offer them help; provide advice when you think it is appropriate; be sensitive to their needs and personal characteristics; and let them know that they can depend on you.

Competition is often the root cause for contention among coworkers. Employees sometimes feel that they are pitted against each other, which often leads to one-upsmanship, back-biting, subtle put-downs, and a chilling atmosphere at work.

The fallacy behind this view of competition is thinking that your success depends on the failure of your coworkers. In reality, your success arises from your professional and personal growth and development, from thoroughly learning your job and doing it effectively and efficiently. The person with whom you compete should be *yourself*.

Try to improve over past performances, find better ways of completing assignments, learn how to use your time more effectively than when you were a novice, challenge yourself to excel in the future.

Avoid The Monster...Especially If It's You

While productivity and performance on the job are important, so too are positive and congenial attitudes. Unfortunately, there are several MONSTERS roaming the workplace that we wish would rapidly become extinct.

The *Blamer Censurius* is a dark, ugly beast destined to live a life of alienation on the job. Since this creature is constantly pointing his claw at others and holding everyone else accountable except himself, no one likes to work with him or be around him. If he makes a mistake, he will never be willing to take responsibility for it. Instead of being seen as a problem solver, as someone who looks for solutions and answers, he constantly searches for ways to distribute or dilute the blame.

The *Protected Posterior*, a member of the turtle family, crawls under a shell and stays there in order to remain safe. "After all," she has been heard to say, "It's a jungle out there." This type of monster will rarely give a coworker a direct answer to any question and usually avoids taking a stand on any issue. Trying anything new or anything whose outcome is uncertain is anathema. However, when the coast is clear, she will emerge and happily take credit for a project's success.

The *Defensive Paranodia*, a creature often found in a frenetic condition, has been heard to cry, "What do you *mean* I made a mistake?" or "No one likes me here." This creature will take all advice and feedback as a personal attack. It is difficult, if not impossible, to communicate with him, for virtually anything anyone says will result in a defensive wail.

The *Complainer Grouse*, a member of the chigger family, is not a life-threatening insect, but causes severe itching and painful irritation of the skin. Her characteristic cries include, "It's not fair;" "I can't believe I got the short end of the stick again;" and "I can't believe what a pittance I am paid." She is convinced that she is the only one in the entire animal kingdom who has ever had bad luck or bad breaks. She sees little that is positive at work and would rather curse at a problem than solve it. She and her specie can be generally recognized by their drooping heads and long faces.

When You Are In Trouble, Ask For Help

"To err," as Alexander Pope said, "is human." Everyone occasionally gets into hot water at work. The key is what you do when you feel the warm bubbles.

The worst mistake is to keep the problem to yourself because you are too proud or too foolish to ask for help. This will often turn a minor problem into a major disaster. Asking for help is not a sign of weakness or the inability to cope; in fact, in firms with enlightened managers, asking for help is generally seen as a sign of maturity and good judgment.

Ask a trusted coworker for advice on how to respond to the problem. If this proves inadequate, explore other courses of action with your boss. One of the primary functions of a manager is to provide this type of advice and assistance to his or her subordinates.

Be Ethical

If you asked employees if they are ethical, most would probably give a knee-jerk response: "Yes, of course I am ethical." That response may well be accurate, but consider the following two scenarios to see if either strikes a familiar chord.

Scenario #1: "It is perfectly acceptable to take home office supplies—e.g., paper, paper clips, pencils, markers—for personal use. After all, everyone does it, and no one's really getting hurt. It's such a small matter." Do you agree or disagree?

In this scenario, the phrase, "After all, everyone does this..." is a frequently used rationalization for unethical or dishonest behavior in the workplace, one based on the illogical position that if many people are bending the rules, then the rules have changed. Most often, however, the rules have NOT changed, and, in this case, what everyone else is doing means precious little when it comes to judging the ethics and honesty of your own behavior.

"...and no one's really getting hurt" is another frequently espoused rationalization. Someone does not have to be hurt for acceptable ethics to be breached. Simply violating a moral principle—in this case, honesty—is both unethical and illegal.

The final rationalization, "It's such a small thing," does not alter the facts of the case. What it *may* alter is the severity of the penalty one receives for stealing. The apparent "triviality" of an unethical act does not make the act any less unethical or illegal.

Scenario #2: You are one desperate manager. You need someone to take on a particularly unpleasant assignment, requiring long hours, a tough client, and extensive travel. And you need someone immediately.

To make the assignment more palatable to a subordinate, you have decided to highlight the few positive aspects of the task and gloss over or omit entirely any discussion of the many negatives. In this way, you reason, you can minimize his resistance to taking on the assignment.

Besides (you're on a rationalization roll now!) this individual is an adult and should be able to see the problems in the assignment without anyone pointing them out to him. Do you agree or disagree with this approach?

Aside from the obvious observation that one should tell the truth, there are two other ethical lessons that may be gleaned from this scenario. First, proper ethical behavior demands that you provide a subordinate with a realistic and honest appraisal of the difficulties and pitfalls of a task. Self-serving motives must be balanced by the employee's right to know what he or she is being asked to do.

Second, ethical behavior does not have to put you at a professional or business disadvantage. A realistic assignment preview generally helps an employee cope with the negative aspects of an assignment and prepare for the contingencies he or she may have to face. Being honest about the nature of an assignment will *increase* the likelihood of its successful completion. Furthermore, withholding needed information will undermine an employee's loyalty to a boss, which may, in turn, adversely affect the productivity of an office.

The following guidelines may help you in making various types of ethical decisions:

Check it out. The working world can at times be an ugly place where people are cajoled, coerced, or "persuaded" to perform an act that may be unethical. If you are not sure what is ethical in a given situation, seek advice and counsel from coworkers, a manager, your firm's human resources staff, or an attorney. You may ask these individuals to keep your request for advice and counsel in confidence.

Monitor yourself. We can get so caught up in our personal achievements and advancement—an issue well depicted in the movie "Wall Street"—that it is possible, perhaps even likely, to forget to ask ourselves if what we are doing is ethically right. Consider how others might perceive the ethics of your actions.

Recognize the value of ethics. It is easy in the sometimes crass and materialistic world of business to forget the value and importance of words such as "integrity," "trust," "honor," and "honesty." The words of Shakespeare are still true and relevant:

Who steals my purse steals trash; 'tis something, nothing;
'Twas mine, 'tis his, and has been slave to thousands;
But he that filches from me my good name
Robs me of that which not enriches him
And makes me poor indeed.

Little Things *Still* Mean A Lot

Small deeds have the potential of taking on remarkable significance. Probably the most effective way, for instance, to build a close and congenial working relationship with your coworkers, boss, or subordinates is also the least time-consuming and least expensive one—saying things like "Thank you;" "I appreciate that;" "That was a fine presentation;" and "Congratulations on a solid piece of work." "I'm sorry;" "I apologize;" and "I was wrong" are among the kindest and most healing words, if not the easiest to utter.

Simple courtesies, such as making coffee when the communal pot is empty, taking phone messages for a coworker, replenishing the supply of paper in the copying machine, and offering to drive someone home when his or her car is being serviced will be repaid bountifully.

Cast your bread upon the waters and it will come back French toast. Kindness is never out of fashion, and it can have a significant impact on the extent of your happiness and success at work.

Some Hints On Getting Promoted

Individuals beginning their career travels can become incredibly impatient about getting promoted. They may watch their boss do his or her job for a few months and quickly assume that they could do it equally as well.

While this may well be true, it does not necessarily mean you are ready for promotion. Your boss has been in the firm longer than you, demonstrated loyalty and commitment to the organization, proved that he or she can handle difficult assignments, and developed through experience a global view of how the firm operates. You, on the other hand, are still a rookie, albeit a talented one.

Be patient and have realistic expectations about promotions and your future. Successful associates in law firms, for instance, struggle for upwards of six to eight years before they make partner.

Physicians do not become full-fledged members of their professional community until they are in their mid-thirties.

Hospital managers generally remain at the assistant level for six years before they become associates.

Academics rarely become full professors before their late forties.

The primary basis for promotion is the quality of your job performance. Learn your job thoroughly and perform it with excellence. If the quality of your work has been merely adequate or mediocre, it is unrealistic to expect your boss to elevate you to a more demanding and complex job.

While learning how to do your current job well, identify and develop the skills and abilities that you will need to perform a job at the next level. While upper management will be most concerned over the quality of your present work, they may also wish to see if you have developed the skills and abilities needed for advancement. Hence, if the next higher job demands negotiating skills, you may wish to develop those skills now—reading books on that topic, attending workshops, taking classes.

Finally, make your achievements and newly developed skills and abilities visible in a tasteful fashion. Inform your boss about projects that have gone well, ideas you have for improved productivity and efficiency in your unit, and professional training that you are receiving. Subtle and diplomatic self-marketing is not out of place, as long as it is tastefully and intelligently disseminated.

Learn The Reward System In Your Organization

All organizations have a formal reward system—to be promoted or to be successful in an organization you must fulfill the requirements of that system. These requirements are generally easy to identify, for they may be communicated to you verbally by your boss, especially in annual goal-setting sessions, or expressed in your letter of appointment.

Many firms, however, also have an *informal* or *unstated* reward system that is equally or more influential. Generally, the criteria of this system are more difficult to identify. In academia, for instance, one is often told that promotion depends on excellence in both teaching and publication. While that may be the official policy for promotion, the reality is that at many institutions teaching is not as important as publication.

In law firms, the *formal* reward system may value excellence in legal research and courtroom presentation. But in reality, the failure to bring new clients to the firm may prevent one from becoming a partner.

You should not ignore the formal reward system; in fact, first and foremost, make sure you satisfy all of the *formal* criteria for promotion. But it is equally important that you also carefully identify the informal or unstated achievements that define high job performance, and thus promotion, in your organization.

Identifying the informal or unstated reward system may be difficult, but there are some things you can do.

First, observe the achievements and qualifications of individuals who are being promoted, then determine if their achievements and qualifications fully reflect the criteria of the *formal* reward system. If their achievements and qualifications differ from the criteria of the formal reward system, and you can observe this pattern in several instances, you may have identified some of the *informal* criteria for promotion in your firm.

Second, be attentive to the behaviors and accomplishments that your boss stresses when he or she gives you positive feedback on your work. If he or she focuses on behaviors and accomplishments different from the criteria of the formal reward system, you may also have identified the informal criteria for promotion

Finally, the informal reward system is a part of the culture of a firm. Learning that culture is vital to your success and fulfillment at work. Conferring with more experienced coworkers, listening to the remarks of various managers, and watching carefully the events transpiring around you are prudent steps in learning your firm's culture.

Seek Evaluation Of Your Work

We spoke in the last chapter of the importance of receiving periodic evaluations of your work. If your firm does not have a formal system of periodic evaluation, *ask* your boss for one.

There are, in addition to *explicit* statements about your work, *implicit* indicators of your performance. Being sensitive to them may tell you as much about your progress as a formal review:

Non-verbal cues: Do people grimace or appear impatient when you present ideas at meetings? Or do they appear to be genuinely listening to what you have to say?

Assignments: Are you getting your share of choice assignments? Or are you always asked to play a back-up or support role to others, even though you have been on the job for a reasonable amount of time?

Involvement: Do people ever come to you for help and advice? Are you asked to attend key meetings and to participate in important activities?

The remarks of others: Are you hearing comments such as: "I've heard good things about you;" "Your boss tells me you are adapting well;" "I understand that you are often given the most difficult problems to solve?"

Consider The Consequences Of Your Actions

Mistakes often occur because individuals fail to understand the full implications of their actions. You may have thought it was a wonderful idea to call on a coworker's client because your work brought you to the client's office building. Your coworker, however, may view this as an attempt to steal a client.

If you had thought through all the implications of your action, you should have been able to see how even a courtesy call could be misinterpreted. It would have been appropriate to ask for permission from your coworker to call on his or her client.

Before acting, examine the implications of your act from numerous perspectives. If you're uncertain of your assessment, discuss the issue with your coworkers or boss. They may be able to point out consequences you never realized.

Learn How To Use Learning Resources

The explosion of knowledge in all fields has made it incumbent upon any employee who wishes to work effectively and efficiently and to remain current in his or her field to know where and how to access information quickly. There are numerous types of learning resources which you should learn how to use: reports from governmental agencies, professional books and journals, research volumes housed in libraries, data bases, computer software, and, of course, knowledgeable colleagues and former teachers.

Knowing how to use the learning resources in your field will help you achieve the job success that you desire. Knowing how to use a library, for instance, or what government agency to call for information, will spare you from spending enormous amounts of time and energy collecting data that has already been gathered.

Knowing how to use learning resources will help you research projects more thoroughly and identify judicious courses of action.

Knowing how to use learning resources will help you to answer questions and gather data independently—you will not have to worry that you are asking your colleagues and boss for an excessive amount of assistance.

We live in an age of rapidly expanding knowledge, which is making most jobs increasingly complex and sophisticated. You will not be able to remain on the cutting edge in your field without knowing how to access many types of information.

Develop A Support System

One of the best resources available to you is a support system of friends, family, and coworkers. Everyone needs people to whom he or she can turn to vent frustrations, to talk about disappointments, to ask for advice, and to seek solace.

At times you will need professional counsel which you can only receive from a colleague; at times you will need personal guidance which you can only receive from a close friend. Coworkers, friends, and family help us to enjoy the mountain tops and cope with the valleys. Cultivate a support system and cherish it.

Plan For The Future

While enjoying the present, prepare for the future. No one is immune from layoffs, buy-outs, or shutdowns. Evaluate the strength of your firm today and try to project its viability five or ten years into the future. Be sensitive to business trends and changing demographics that could affect your firm.

Keep your working skills updated by reading trade publications, attending professional seminars, and staying abreast of the latest technological developments in your field. Develop secondary interests that could be shaped into a career. Self-development will not only help you do your current job better, but also increase your marketability and attractiveness to other employers.

The fifteen recommendations in this chapter are not, of course, the sum total of what one has to know and do to succeed at work. You will develop, through the millennia-old method of trial and error, your own strategies for dealing with bosses and peers, clients and kooks, successes and setbacks, and the myriad of unforeseen and unexpected events that make the workplace so exciting.

Seven

MEN AND WOMEN IN THE WORKPLACE

The New Demographics

When comparing the workplace of your parents to the workplace that you are in, one major difference shines as brightly as a super nova: A major social revolution is occurring, and women are at the heart of it. According to Randall S. Schuler, author of <u>Personnel and Human Resources Management</u>:

- In the 1950s, approximately 60% of American families contained a male breadwinner and a female homemaker. Today only 20% of American families fit this profile.

- Currently both spouses work in about two-thirds of American households, regardless of income level.

- Nearly half of all mothers with children under five work outside the home.

- It is estimated that in 1990, 80% of all women in their primary childbearing years will be working.

- The Census Bureau estimates that nearly half of the nation's new mothers hold jobs or are looking for jobs within a year of the birth of their child.
- 30% of the students in degree programs in business school are women.
- In 1970, 43% of this country's women were employed outside of their homes. By 1995, the number is expected to reach 60%.
- Currently women comprise approximately 44% of the American work force.

These demographics suggest that men and women are currently working together and will continue to do so in the future to a much greater extent than has ever occurred in the past. Understanding the challenges of the new workplace are essential if you are to work effectively with and for women, regardless of your gender.

Some Issues That Women Face

Should I try to act like my male coworkers or just be myself?

Rather than thinking in terms of acting like a man or a woman, you would be better served to think in terms of acting like a professional. Being a professional means dealing with the men and women you encounter in a business fashion first, in a business fashion second, and in a business fashion third. This does not mean that you have to be standoffish or aloof, but it does mean that favoritism, bias, or partiality should not be shown to one gender. Interactions with coworkers should be congenial and pleasant but should be kept at a professional level.

It is the nature of your job and the tasks you are asked to perform, and not your gender, that should dictate how you behave. If you are working, for instance, in a traditionally conservative field, such as banking or healthcare, your dress, demeanor, and behavior should be consistent with the norms and expectations of that field. If you are working in a less conservative field, such as advertising or public relations, their norms and expectations may permit more latitude in your dress, demeanor, and behavior.

Acting in a professional manner also means being yourself. If hunkering down with colleagues is your style, then go ahead and hunker down. If that would make you feel uncomfortable, then avoid doing it. If you have a sprightly personality, do not try to suffocate it. If you are by nature reticent and conservative, do not suddenly start wearing a lamp shade.

Let people see and accept the real you. To try to be someone you are not will result in a phoniness as transparent as cellophane. It will alienate your coworkers and, more importantly, it will displease you. If the firm you work for expects you to give up being who you are, you may want to reevaluate your decision to work there.

How should I respond to gender insensitivity?

Since the demographic changes in the workplace are fairly recent, it should not be surprising to find vestiges of sexism. How you respond to such attitudes, which can range from being asked to make coffee for a morning meeting to sexual harassment, is a subjective matter. Be true to yourself. Respond to sexist behavior when you feel that your dignity or self-esteem has been violated. But when you do respond, do so with tact and professionalism. Statements such as, "I feel uncomfortable hearing stereotypic sexist jokes," send a clear message and minimize the chances of damaging a working relationship.

However, in the imperfect world of the workplace, responding to minor sexist behavior may well have a negative effect on your relationship with coworkers. Before expressing your displeasure, think carefully of the consequences, both good and bad, of your response.

More serious matters, such as sexual harassment, lower pay, or being denied professional advancement, demand a more serious approach. Try to solve the problem initially at the level at which it occurred. If you believe that you are not being treated equitably by your boss, discuss this matter with him or her in a professional, non-threatening manner.

If the problem cannot be resolved at this level, then you may wish to proceed to the human resources office in your firm. In the absence of such a department (the case in many smaller and even some mid-sized companies), it may be necessary for you to confidentially discuss the problem with your boss's boss.

If you still are not satisfied that the problem has been resolved, the next step is either to consult a labor attorney or to leave the firm. Before taking this radical measure, discuss the matter with trusted coworkers and friends and carefully weigh both the positive and negative consequences of your decision.

Should I try to find female mentors?

It is important to enlist the support of women who have been in your unit or firm for some time. They can advise you on gender issues in terms of the culture of the firm; they can apprise you of potential personnel problems; they can advise you on your manner of dress and behavior; they can inform you of problems they have faced in the firm.

Men, of course, should also be a part of your support network, but if you are fortunate enough to find women mentors, your adjustment to a job should be greatly facilitated.

Can I have a successful career and a successful personal life?

The answer is,"Yes," *if* you are willing to make compromises and trade-offs. Starting a career takes a great deal of time and energy. It should not be surprising that your social life will not be as active as it was when you were in school. Play time, however, is important to your physical and psychological well being and should not be overlooked. The key is to maintain a healthy balance among your varied interests and responsibilities—paying attention to each, ignoring none.

One of the compromises that many women entering the work force have made is to delay starting a family until they have more control over their careers and work schedules. In 1970, for instance, approximately 4% of women waited until they were 30 or older to have children; today that figure has increased to approximately 16%.

Numerous other compromises may also be made. Some women, wishing to have more time to spend with a spouse or children, have opted for part-time or flex-time working schedules.

Increasingly, men have subordinated their careers so that their spouses can maximize their own professional growth.

As you enter the workplace, it is important to have realistic expectations of what you can accomplish in both your professional and personal life. Trying to be "Superwoman" will only result in enormous stress and frustration. Compromises, trade-offs, and concessions are not cop-outs; they are the very bases of a satisfying professional and personal life.

Guidelines For Men Working With And For Women

As we noted earlier, the changing demographics of the workplace suggest that it is increasingly likely that a male employee is either currently working with or for a woman or will be in the near future.

The following quiz is designed to help men assess how prepared they are to work with or for women. Circle your responses to each question, grading yourself on a scale from 5 ("strongly agree") to 1 ("strongly disagree").

1. It is appropriate to refer to secretaries as "girls."

    5   4   3   2   1

2. It is appropriate for me to give my female coworker or boss a congratulatory kiss on the cheek after she has completed a major project or closed an important deal.

5   4   3   2   1

3. Men and women at work may be attracted to one another. If I were attracted to my female coworker or boss, I don't think it would be improper to ask her for a date.

5   4   3   2   1

4. Since men are generally responsible for the financial welfare of a family, I don't think that a woman's career is as important as a man's career.

5   4   3   2   1

5. While women in their '20s may care about their careers, I feel that they are generally not as interested as men in long-range career goals.

5   4   3   2   1

6. While I do not mind working for women, I would prefer to be supportive of a male coworker or boss as opposed to a female coworker or boss.

5   4   3   2   1

7. While a female may be competent, I suspect that I would have to shield her from difficult business problems to a greater extent than I would a male.

5   4   3   2   1

8. I think women should be sophisticated enough not to object to an occasional "dirty" or "off-color" joke, as long as it is not directed at them.

5   4   3   2   1

9. I believe that women are, more often than not, intellectually and emotionally less capable than men of assuming leadership positions.

5   4   3   2   1

The lower your total score, the better prepared you are to work with and for women. A score in the vicinity of 27 or higher suggests that you may benefit from reading the following section. Even a score of 4 or 5 on a single question may indicate the need to consider the advice below.

In an effort to determine what types of attitudes and behavior women desire from their male coworkers or subordinates, we asked a number of working women what advice and recommendations they would like to pass along to men. The following guidelines are the result.

What Women Want Men To Know And Do

Avoid sexism and sexist behavior.

There is no guideline that we can emphasize more than this one. In many, if not most, cases, sexism or sexist behavior is not conscious or deliberate. It is a pattern of conduct that has been so ingrained in the psyche of many males that it is done unintentionally and without premeditation. This does *not*, however, excuse it, for it is a pattern of behavior that is patronizing and humiliating to women.

Sexist language, such as referring to women, be they executives or members of the clerical staff, as "girls" or "the girls," must be avoided. "Ladies" is a more polite term, but still can be denigrating with the wrong inflection. They are *women*.

The entire range of sexist linguistic practices must also be eschewed: using only masculine references in your speech ("Let's put our best man in our branch office," when you really mean our best "person"); using only the masculine pronoun "he" in your examples ("This business is a place where he can rise to the top level of management in five years," when you really mean that "one" can rise to the top level); giving examples that are in themselves sexist ("We have the same spirit in this office that you'd find on a tough football team").

Males showing preference, even subtly, to male colleagues must be avoided—including only males in after-hours social or professional activities; trivializing the personal and professional contributions or achievements of women in comparison to similar accomplishments by men; ignoring at meetings the responses of women, while giving rapt attention to the comments of men; not treating questions or requests from women as seriously as you do those from men; having different standards of achievement for women and men; singling out women, never men, as the butt of jokes.

While humor and laughter help us get through the day (Mark Twain said that humans are the only animals who laugh—or *have* to), a great deal of care and sensitivity should be taken in the selection of jokes. Sexual jokes are almost always at the expense of women: they are demeaning, embarrassing, dehumanizing, and ugly.

Even though you may not intend to direct a sexist or dirty joke at the women in your presence, they have every right to be offended. If you are in doubt whether a joke is in bad taste, don't tell it.

Avoid patronizing physical acts.

It is sometimes difficult to determine where politeness stops and condescension begins. Standing up when a women enters the room or opening a car door is polite. Offering to carry a woman's attache case crosses the line into condescension.

Physical gestures of approbation or congratulations, such as putting your arm around your coworker's or boss's shoulder when she has successfully negotiated a large contract, giving her a hug, or kissing her cheek, should be avoided.

As with most rules of thumb, there are exceptions. Your understanding of the audience—how your female coworkers and boss will respond to physical gestures of approbation or congratulations—may suggest that a hug or a kiss on the cheek would not be inappropriate. If in doubt, however, it is advisable to bridle your enthusiasm. A smile or handshake can send as thoughtful a message as a hug and kiss—with less danger of being taken the wrong way.

Be as supportive of your female coworker or boss as you would be of a male coworker or boss.

Even though you may not feel totally comfortable with what you consider to be a role-reversal, letting your female colleagues know that you are there to assist them and that they can always depend on your goodwill and hard work will be beneficial to them, the firm, and yourself.

We hope that by understanding the sense of isolation many females experi-ence and by recognizing the sense of uncertainty and doubt caused by the absence of mentors, male employees will be encouraged to be supportive.

Do not be overprotective of your female coworker or boss.

There is, of course, a difference between being supportive and being overprotective. Implicit in a number of the interviews we conducted is the notion that women wish to be treated the same as men—they simply want an *equal* chance to win or to lose on the job.

When bad news occurs, there is no reason to withhold it from your female coworkers or boss; they are readily equipped and willing to handle it.

When dirty work needs to be done, do not assume that women are unwilling to do it.

Occasionally male subordinates may protect their female coworkers and boss in subtle, even unconscious, ways. A male employee may fail to tell his female coworker or boss that he has arranged a 9:00 dinner with an important client because he believes that she may feel compelled to attend, and that this would create a role conflict for her between family responsibilities and the demands of the business.

He has taken responsibility for making a decision away from her, while attributing to her what he assumes would be a conflict of values.

This type of protective behavior, albeit well intentioned, is inappropriate and gratuitous.

Assume that a woman is* at least *as competent as a man.

A typical syllogism reflecting the reluctance of a man to work for a woman he assumes is incompetent may resemble the following:

> Proposition 1: *Women bosses are incompetent.*
>
> Proposition 2: *If I work for a woman boss, I will be seen as incompetent.*
>
> Conclusion: *I should not work for a woman boss.*

The fallacy in this syllogism, of course, is assuming that a woman is any less talented, capable, or competent than a man. In fact, if a woman has achieved a leadership position, she probably faced *more* obstacles and had to prove her abilities to a *greater* degree than a man.

The question is not so much the *reality* of competence as the *perception* of competence. Males often receive from an early age the prejudice that competence is more closely associated with men than with women. G.I. Joe, for instance, reeks of achievement, accomplishment, and success; those characteristics are irrelevant to a Barbie doll.

While women in the workplace may be as talented as men, the paucity of women in top corporate positions has denied them the opportunity of establishing highly visible role models or a long tradition of talented executives. We urge men to realize that ability, competence, and talent are gender-free.

Respect your female boss's desire to maintain a social distance.

Respect your female supervisor's desire to keep her male employees both literally and figuratively at arm's length, and avoid imposing on whatever social distance she wishes to maintain.

Susan J., an unmarried corporate vice-president, told us that she constantly monitors her social relationships with employees: "For the men I manage in particular, I must make sure that I stay at arm's length (no pun intended). This isn't always easy; I like men. Just the other day a new male employee in an entry-level position came to work. He's a hunk: 6'2", deep blue eyes, and gorgeous blond hair. But I had to put my libido on hold.

"As it turned out, he was also interested in me. Eventually he asked another employee what my first name was. The employee responded, 'Her first name is vice-president.' That tells you how vigilant I am about social distance. I get the word out and then other employees spread it. I have no choice in the matter, for I would completely undermine my credibility and effectiveness if people got the impression that I'm in a relationship with a male employee."

It is never a good idea to ask your boss for a date. Asking her to a business lunch, however, is not only permissible but appropriate and advisable. Asking her for drinks or dinner after work is also acceptable, as long as the focus of the conversation is professionally oriented and the intent is not romance.

The natural human urge to know about a person's personal life must be controlled. In the unlikely, yet possible, event that your female boss wishes to discuss her marriage or her social life, try to maintain as much social distance as possible. The consequences of knowing too much about people with whom you work may be more harmful than not knowing anything about them.

Assume that a woman is as serious about her career as a man is about his.

Decisions in the workplace are sometimes based on the implicit and unspoken assumptions that a woman does not desire to have a lifelong career or that she, in general, is not as serious about her career as her male counterparts. This view of women as glorified part-time or temporary workers may create serious problems of inequity:

- A plum assignment may be given to a male instead of a female manager on the erroneous assumption

that he has a greater commitment to building a
career.

- Based on the same specious reasoning, a male
  manager may be promoted to a higher level in the
  organization than a comparable female.

- Company funds may be more likely to be allocated
  for the training and development of men than of
  women.

Top management may be more willing, for instance, to send a young male executive to a Harvard
University Advanced Management program because he is perceived as having a long-term
commitment to a career, while a woman manager
is seen as a more transitory figure, working only
until she decides to get married or raise a family.

It is imperative to realize that women can be just as committed to their careers as men.

Guidelines For Women Working With and For Women

While the number of men working with and for women
over the next ten years will increase, so too will the number of
women working with and for women.

Although on the surface this change may not seem
difficult, it is fraught with problems as complex as those
experienced by men.

The magnitude of the difficulty is suggested in a
nationwide poll conducted by Kathleen Parker which found
that nearly half of the women surveyed did not want to work
for other women.

The following guidelines will assist female employees in
working with and for women.

Respect the career goals of your female coworkers and boss.

Obviously not all people have the same goals in the workplace. Some women wish to pursue a career as an end in itself, as a means of obtaining personal and professional fulfillment and satisfaction. Others are not career oriented, but look upon a job as a means to an end, a way of paying the bills or getting the children through college. It is important for women in both groups to understand and respect each others' goals.

A difficulty they may experience in doing this is based on the psychological fallacy called "false consensus bias"—the belief that others feel exactly the same as you do about specific issues. A non-career woman must realize the strength of her coworker's or boss's commitment to the missions and objectives of the firm, her professional interests, and her concerns, even anxieties, over the future of her career. The career woman, conversely, must realize that some, if not many, of her female colleagues do not share her allegiance or her career interests.

A female boss must accept the fact that her subordinates may have been shaped by environmental factors and life experiences that have left them with an entirely different set of priorities. Value judgments are inappropriate. There is no moral imperative—no right or wrong—in these matters. Each individual must be true to herself and accept the legitimacy of differing values.

Be supportive of your female coworkers and boss.

Women in the workplace often experience a sense of isolation because of the absence of female mentors in their professional lives. This places a responsibility on the shoulders of female employees to provide vital psychological, professional, and moral support for each other. They may offer assistance and advice, for instance, for dealing with gender issues in the workplace: how to manage a recalcitrant male employee, how to overcome the resentment of a male who dislikes working with or for a female, how to avoid nepotism without discriminating against women, or how to avoid creating a provocative sartorial image.

Do not look upon your boss as a mother figure.

The "mother-figure syndrome" may take several forms, but there are two manifestations that are most common.

Some female subordinates have difficulty working for a woman boss because it forces them to relive conflicts they may have had with their mothers. Psychologist Harry Levinson, in his book, Executive Stress, theorizes that women who work for women may unconsciously be reminded of the difficulties they experienced when they were attempting to assert their personal identity during their adolescent years.

Under this scenario, the female subordinate will tend to view her female boss as a mother figure who, like her real mother, may seek to impede the expression of her individualism and adulthood. "Mom" becomes the nay-sayer, the villainous adversary standing in the way of her personal freedom.

The female subordinate who experiences this reenactment of her adolescent years will likely view the leadership style of her boss as overly directive, will chafe at her boss's efforts to guide her, and will interpret constructive criticism or benign feedback as an attempt to exert control.

A second way in which this syndrome may be manifested is in a female subordinate's excessive dependence on her female boss. She may go to her to discuss personal problems, to ask for advice on social matters, and to seek from her—as one would from a mother—emotional comfort and support.

While a woman boss may well understand the nature of the problems and issues being brought to her, time pressures and work demands may limit her ability to respond to them as sensitively as a mother would.

We recommend that a female subordinate who falls into this group respect the range of responsibilities faced by her boss.

Do not expect to be treated in a preferential manner because you and your boss are of the same gender.

Women should not assume that since they, like their bosses, are members of an "oppressed majority," they will automatically receive preferential treatment. Women managers are painfully aware that they are both in the spotlight and under the microscope. Their attitudes, decisions, and behaviors are constantly being scrutinized and evaluated.

Women managers who wish to maintain their effectiveness in a firm will be certain that they are not seen as proponents or practitioners of nepotism. They realize that their success depends to a great extent on a loyal and committed work force. To alienate a large segment of that work force (the men) by displays of—or even the impression of—favoritism or reverse discrimination would be to commit career suicide.

Ironically, the desire to avoid charges of favoritism may prompt a female manager to *over*compensate, to be *more* demanding of her female subordinates than of her male employees. Like the son who ends up cleaning the bathrooms because his dad owns the business, female subordinates may find that working for a woman has more drawbacks than working for a man. According to Kathleen Parker, who has studied the relationship between women bosses and their subordinates, "No one is harder on women than other women."

A classic example of a female manager who failed to keep gender out of a personnel decision was recently brought to our attention. A woman was hired as president of a company after her female predecessor moved to the presidency of another firm. The executive vice president, a male, had done outstanding work under the predecessor. During his tenure, the company expanded significantly during a period of enormous instability in their industry.

The new president, according to our male and female sources for this case, did not feel comfortable having men in her top management group. Within weeks of her arrival, she fired the successful male executive vice president and replaced him with a new female executive, an act which raised more than a few eyebrows.

The male was not out of work very long. When his former boss learned what had happened, she hired him immediately.

The moral of this story is *not,* "Women are less competent than men," but rather, "If it ain't broke, don't fix it." Finding successful executive talent is not easy. The new female executive took a foolish risk by firing an established winner. To do so on the basis of gender simply compounded the mistake.

The message from female managers to their female employees that we continuously hear is clear and direct: Good human resources are hard enough to find; limiting themselves to only one gender is hazardous both to their careers and to the company's health. High job performance will be rewarded, regardless of one's gender.

The Gender-Free Workplace

Should we work toward the goal of "degenderizing" the workplace? In its starkest form, this concept holds that the workplace should be totally gender-free. One should not, for instance, think in terms of a female office manager or male office manager, but rather in terms of an office manager. A man or a woman is not hired; a person is hired.

Not only should we treat men and women impartially and equally, but we must also interact with men and women, speak to them, respond to them, and even think of them in identical terms.

We understand the historical circumstances that have led to this concept. There are groups that have been traditionally the victims of discrimination, and it is vital that all vestiges of discriminatory treatment and stereotyping be removed from the workplace. Equality, fairness, and equity must be assiduously practiced, not merely because it is the law, but also because it is morally and ethically correct.

While much has been accomplished, we still have a long way to go before we achieve genuine equality in the workplace. That will have happened when we no longer say, "I hired a woman today," or "I promoted a Black today," or "I gave a raise to a handicapped person today," but state instead that an outstanding person was hired or promoted or given a raise.

We are not convinced, however, that it is realistic or even possible to remove gender totally from the workplace—to interact with, relate to, or think about an individual without reference to gender. Nor do we think it is inappropriate to admire a man's or a woman's physical appearance any more than it is inappropriate to admire his or her wit or charm or sensitivity. We do not believe that one should feel guilt-ridden or unprofessional if he or she becomes conscious of the figure or physique or sex appeal of a coworker or boss.

The workplace is not populated by automatons but by flesh-and-blood people with emotions, sensibilities, and passions. The important issue is not that one must deny these personal impressions or feelings, but that one must keep them separate from the professional evaluation, treatment, and judgment of an individual.

Such a separation is, of course, more facilely achieved in theory than in practice; it is an easy matter to allow comeliness and attractiveness, as well as a host of other attributes, to affect our decisions. The complexity of interactions that occur in the workplace demands that we remain self-consciously vigilant to avoid allowing our personal predilections, prejudices, and preferences to influence our professional judgment and conduct.

The Supportive Workplace

Most of us, we suspect, would feel uncomfortable thinking of the workplace as a huge "touchy-feelie" adult playpen where everyone feels compelled to have a "totally honest" relationship with everyone else.

Yet, a major revolution is occurring in the workplace, and it would seem to be in the best interests of both men and women to share their feelings, biases, and expectations in an open and organized manner. Women's support groups, workshops on the relationship between men and women in the workplace, seminars on unconscious discrimination or sexual harassment—to name only a few activities—may help men and women to appreciate and resolve mutual problems occasioned by the influx of women into the work force. At the very least, they encourage people to talk to one another about transitional matters.

There are numerous options and programs—day care assistance, flexible working hours, job sharing—that should be explored by corporate America to help employees balance their professional and personal lives. A female non-manager who is committed to her family will undoubtedly be a more effective employee if she knows that her children are being properly cared for at the company's day care facility. A female manager committed to both her family and her career may be able to avoid an emotional conflict if her firm provides child-care support tailored to the demands of her job.

Employee assistance programs, which are burgeoning throughout the United States, are excellent vehicles for offering individual counseling to help male and female managers and non-managers adjust to these changes.

Women are entering the work force in extraordinary numbers. The corporations that will flourish in the future will be the ones that confront, understand, nurture, and support this transition.

Eight

THE WRONG REASONS
FOR STAYING AT
OR LEAVING A JOB

Humans are curious animals—we are rarely satisfied with the status quo. Soon after settling into a new job and becoming comfortable with our new surroundings, we begin to cast our eyes to what seem like greener pastures.

Although the trend is slowing, James D. Kohlman, author of <u>Make Them Choose You: The Executive Selection Process,</u> notes that white-color employees typically will change jobs seven to eight times during their working years.

How long *should* you stay at any one job? What *are* the right and wrong reasons for moving? How *do* you judge if you have a future in a company? How *do* you evaluate a job offer? In this chapter and the next, we shall address these and other related questions.

Jim S. had been looking forward to his fifth-year college reunion for months. It would be a time of nostalgia and sentiment; a time for renewing old friendships and taking stock of himself.

He returned from the reunion in a state of abject depression and bitter frustration. For an entire weekend, he was

regaled by his former classmates with tales of their successes: the catamaran purchased by his fraternity brother;
the mail order business founded by his former roommate; the
recent promotion and overseas assignment of the woman he
took to his senior prom.

While Jim always had been reasonably satisfied with his
job, he was suddenly filled with doubt and dissatisfaction. His
salary, which had never troubled him before, now seemed
paltry. The fact that he shared a secretary with a colleague
became intolerably demeaning. Innocuous memos from his
boss became poison pen letters. Perfunctory remarks from his
coworkers were acrimonious put-downs.

As his job dissatisfaction increased, it turned into para-
noia: He was surrounded by disloyal coworkers, superiors
who exploited him, and hidden agendas designed to discredit
him. Life at work became unbearable. He accepted the only
solution that occurred or appealed to him—he began to look
for another job.

There is nothing inherently wrong with changing jobs.
The notion of being "married" to one's job is an unfortunate
metaphor, for it creates an impression of betrayal or desertion
if one seeks new employment. There are numerous viable,
sensible, even compelling, reasons for changing jobs.

According to a 1987 poll conducted by *USA Today*, 52% of
the respondents said that they now work in a different field
(not simply a different job) than the one they planned to go into
when they finished school. It is important, therefore, that you
be able to identify and understand the right *and* the wrong
reasons for changing jobs.

Jim S. committed three cardinal errors:

1) He did not evaluate his current job situation
dispassionately, and comprehensively;

2) He did not seek specific and substantive information on the nature of his friends' work; and

3) he did not make comparisons between himself and others based on analogous information.

The Wrong Reasons For
Staying At Your Job

All job changes should begin with an accurate and honest assessment of your current working situation. That assessment may begin by examining the following seven statements frequently heard in the marketplace. Read each statement carefully, and then answer "true" if the statement applies to you or "false" if it does not.

1. I am staying at my current job primarily because I am frightened of being rejected by other employers. I would like to move on, but I can't stand the thought of coming home to letters of rejection.

TRUE _____   FALSE _____

2. I am staying at my current job primarily because I fear my boss would learn of my job search and treat me shabbily for my perceived disloyalty.

TRUE _____   FALSE _____

3. I am staying at my current job because it is finally feeling comfortable. A new job would mean meeting new people, learning the peculiarities of a new boss, acquiring new job skills, and beginning all over again the entire process of acclimation. The thought of change causes my blood to run cold.

TRUE _____   FALSE _____

4. I am staying at my current job out of loyalty to my employer. She took a risk in hiring me when I was a rookie, and I feel I owe something to her.

TRUE _____   FALSE _____

5. I am staying at my current job, even though I am not particularly happy, because work is merely a means to an end. It allows me to pay my bills and to

maintain my lifestyle. Anyone who thinks work can be pleasurable is not in touch with reality.

TRUE _____   FALSE _____

6. I am staying at my current job primarily because I cannot afford the financial burden of changing jobs. When I consider the cost of a new home in a more expensive geographical area, mortgage rates, and moving expenses, I estimate that I would initially suffer a 20% to 30% reduction in salary.

TRUE _____   FALSE _____

7. I am staying at my current job, even though I do not like it, because I am not yet very marketable. I will hang by my thumbs for a few years until I have gained the seasoning that I need to land a really good job.

TRUE _____   FALSE _____

If your primary reason for staying at your current job is reflected in any of these statements, you may be doing yourself a disservice. While we readily admit that in some cases they may constitute valid reasons for maintaining the status quo, they may also be seen as rationalizations—ostensibly logical and attractive—used for justifying inertia.

Each statement represents a negative rather than a positive reason for remaining where you are. If you believe that you are creating artificial barriers to a potential successful change, looking at what each of these statements says about you may help you take charge of your life.

Fear of Rejection

It is entirely natural that we should wish to seek pleasure and avoid pain. Some pain, however, generally in the form of rejection, is inextricably linked to any job search and must be accepted as going with the territory. While the ratio of rejections to acceptances varies substantially by field and level of training, a general rule of thumb, according to Richard Bolles, is that for every 100 resumes that are sent out, one to four interviews will be granted. On the average, three interviews will result in one job offer.

Furthermore, job-related rejection should be kept in proper perspective: Your feelings of self worth should *not* be equated with the ability to secure a job. There are many reasons why would-be employees are turned down—virtually none of them has to do with the value of the applicant as a human being. Throughout the job-to-job transition, it's easy to discount psychologically your skills and abilities. Do not fall into this self-demeaning trap.

Fear Of Your Employer Finding Out

This fear, while at times very real, should not deter you. Job searches may be conducted with total privacy—simply request in your cover letter to a potential employer that you wish your application to be held in confidence. Reiterate this when you speak to him or her. It is certainly acceptable to list as references individuals not associated with your current firm.

If your potential new employer *does* contact your present employer—and, yes, it does happen—it would probably (and hopefully) occur at a point near the consummation of a job offer. In this case, such an inquiry may well increase your prestige, stature, and value in the eyes of your current boss. Being a sought-after employee is a compliment to you as well as to the individual who had the wisdom to hire you.

If you have heard coworkers speak disparagingly of individuals who have "flown the coop," it may be beneficial to examine the origins of these remarks. Sometimes they reflect a degree of envy and jealousy in the hen house. Often negative comments constitute a self-serving ploy on the part of the speaker to preserve his or her own self-esteem and ego, while validating his or her decision to stay.

Fear Of The New And Unfamiliar

We are all creatures of comfort, especially psychological comfort. We like being surrounded by people we know and enjoy. We relish the feeling of having mastered the intricacies of our jobs. We enjoy working in a familiar environment. But when comfort—and not the quality of the job—becomes the main reason for staying, "comfort" can become a debilitating concept.

Change implies a certain amount of disruption, doubt, and risk, but those troublesome feelings should be offset by the potential benefits of a new job. Without the willingness to endure a degree of anxiety, second thoughts, and cold feet, one would never be able to overcome inertia. The thought of change is often much worse than the reality.

Fear Of Disappointing Your Current Employer

Feelings of loyalty to an employer are not just appropriate, they are laudable. Seeking a new job, however, is not an act of contempt or ingratitude. It is an attempt to give oneself the opportunity to grow and develop. It should be looked upon as a natural occurrence in one's professional life.

If a job move has been thoroughly analyzed, if the reasons are valid, if your departure is done in an ethical and professional manner, your employer will most likely not only understand your decision, but wish you well. You may, by the way, be surprised at how well your former firm adjusts to your departure.

It Is Better To Be A Martyr Than To Move

As illogical and self-defeating as it sounds, there are those who would rather suffer "the slings and arrows of outrageous fortune" than "take arms" and seek a better position.

There are sundry reasons why people remain at unrewarding jobs. For some, it is because they have a negative self-image and conclude that they do not deserve anything better. For others, it is the philosophical belief that life is to be much endured and little enjoyed. For still others, it is the sympathy and moral support they receive from colleagues ("You are a real trooper;" "My goodness, how do you endure") when they describe their dismal situation.

In each of these cases, employees are not basing their unwillingness to move on valid reasons. Not only will job-related success and happiness elude them, but their future will be as bleak as their present.

I Cannot Afford To Move

Under some circumstances, this may be a reasonable explanation for not undertaking a job-to-job transition. Or it may be a ruse. Ultimately, it often comes down to a trade-off between your long-term work sanity and professional advancement, on the one hand, and your short-term financial well-being, on the other.

To determine if *you* are engaging in self-deception, ask yourself one question: "Am I better off saving money while staying in a mediocre job with little future or should I use some of my savings to secure a job that has a better chance of making me feel good about myself and my work?"

I Need More Experience Before I Move

If you do not like your present job and there is no end to the horror in sight, look elsewhere, regardless of your experience. You have little to lose, besides a slightly bruised ego, and potentially much to gain. There is always the chance, of course, that you will get lucky and land your dream job.

But even if you fail to find a new job, this testing of the job-market waters will acquaint you with the specific demands of the marketplace, while allowing you to identify concrete weaknesses in your work experience that you can address. Ultimately a more savvy and marketable job candidate will emerge from the experience.

The Wrong Reasons For *Leaving* Your Job

Let's reverse the coin. If those are the wrong reasons for *staying,* what are the wrong reasons for *leaving?*

Below are seven statements. Answer "true" if the statement describes your attitude, "false" if it does not.

1) I read an employment ad in the *Wall Street Journal* that described a job similar to mine at $7,000 more than I am making. I would be foolish not to apply.

TRUE _____   FALSE _____

2) I do not mind what I am doing. In fact, I enjoy work most of the time. But when I compare myself to the people who were my classmates in high school or college, I find that they are doing much better than I. They are making more money, receiving promotions faster, and buying more adult toys than I am. It has *got* to be better elsewhere.

TRUE _____   FALSE _____

3) Quite honestly, I have had it where I am. The job is no longer challenging; everyone here stifles my creativity and initiative. I can't stand it at work any longer; I am *desperate* to get out of this place.

TRUE _____   FALSE _____

4) Although I basically like what I do, everyone tells me that I am too good for this job, that I should

have a job with more status and prestige. I think I will look elsewhere so that I can fulfill my destiny.

TRUE _____   FALSE _____

5) I am so frustrated that I have got to get out of this job. I'm getting no support from management or my coworkers. I try to get things accomplished, but other people keep getting in my way. It *can't* be like this in other companies.

TRUE _____   FALSE _____

6) I have given a lot to my company and have received very little in return. I *know* that I would be treated better elsewhere.

TRUE _____   FALSE _____

7) Lately things have not been going very well for me. Just the other day I had a problem that seemed as if it would never get resolved. True, I have had my share of success here, but every once in a while a problem emerges, and I think that I am going to go crazy. It has *got* to be better elsewhere.

TRUE _____   FALSE _____

While these statements may represent valid reasons for looking elsewhere, the attitudes embodied in them can make your current pasture appear falsely brown and pastures elsewhere seem as green as artificial turf. They may be poor reasons for making your next career transition.

I Can Make More Money Elsewhere

The possibility of a higher salary excites the avaricious instincts in all of us. As the old bromide goes, "Rich or poor, it's nice to have money."

Money is important, especially during the early months and years of your career. But it should not be the primary basis for a change of jobs. A successful job has many components—a sense of fulfillment, a feeling of professional growth that results from being challenged, supportive bosses, amiable colleagues, a comfortable work environment, the satisfaction of achievement, a variety of assignments, a degree of autonomy, and room for advancement. A sufficient salary is one of those components—*just one*—and it does not rank near the top.

In the 1987 *USA Today* poll cited earlier, only 15% of those interviewed responded that money was the most important element they look for in a job; 39% responded that job satisfaction was the single most important component.

Another survey of 5,000 households conducted by a New York City research group was recently reported in the *Columbus Dispatch*. And it produced similar findings: Individuals rated the nature of the work they do as more satisfying and important than their paychecks.

We believe it is extremely shortsighted and imprudent to make a job move without carefully considering *all* the components. A higher salary at the cost of job/goal satisfaction and professional growth is not a wise trade-off.

There is a rule of thumb about salary upgrades that we would like to pass on: A salary increase of up to 20% will *not* significantly affect your lifestyle or standard of living. You won't suddenly be living on easy street, devoid of money worries, enjoying the good life. In fact, precious little will change.

I'm Not Doing As Well As Others

Comparisons between yourself and peers in other firms can be a major cause of job discontentment and the basis for an erroneous decision to seek employment elsewhere. Remember the problems that comparisons between himself and his college friends caused Jim S.?

Making comparisons is, at best, risky business. For comparisons to be valid, they must be based on detailed, comprehensive, and accurate data—a condition that often does not exist. Ego, insecurity, self-aggrandizement, the desire to be admired and respected, are only several of the factors that prevent peers from presenting an accurate and balanced view of their accomplishments and rewards. Stockbrokers, we are asked to believe, never lose money for a client; salesmen never lose an account; teachers never teach a bad class; managers never misread the taste of the public (the Edsel and the "New" Coca-Cola were only figments of our imagination).

Furthermore, salaries are often rounded "up" (e.g. $43,000 suddenly becomes "almost 50 grand"), never down. Bosses are always enthusiastic supporters, never apathetic bystanders. Working conditions are never less than ideal. If you believe *half* of what you are told by peers, then we would like to talk to you about buying a beach umbrella franchise in Antarctica.

The point is that for comparisons to be *meaningful,* you must have accurate and concrete information, the type of information to which you rarely have access.

Moreover, in making comparisons you must be able to put the progress of a peer in the context of the firm and industry in which he or she is employed. Does his or her firm promote junior managers rapidly, only to allow them to languish in middle management positions? Does it start people at relatively high salaries, then award below-average increments? What are the medical, insurance, and retirement benefits it offers? What is the value of the total fiscal package?

These are some of the more obvious fallacies in trying to make comparisons. Ultimately, however, the entire issue is moot. As noted earlier, the person about whom you should be most concerned is you. Why should the fate of others affect you? If you are relatively content, feel good about yourself and the contributions you are making to your firm, and have a sense of accomplishment, then the experience of others—good or bad—does not seem to hold much importance.

If you insist on making comparisons, let them be between yourself now and yourself one year *ago*. Between yourself now and your projected situation one year *from now*.

I Am Desperate To Get Out Of Here

Consider the true story of Tom D. and you will see the fallacy of allowing desperation to cause you to move from one job to another.

In many ways, Tom was succeeding in his job at the bank. In an industry notorious for slow promotion, he was on a "fast track." He had moved from management trainee to assistant branch manager to branch manager to assistant vice president of commercial investments in record time.

Still, he had an entrepreneurial streak which he could not express in an industry as conservative as banking. Frustrated by his unsatisfied need for creativity and innovation, he started looking for employment elsewhere. He even had several headhunters looking for him. Within a few months, a number of opportunities had emerged, but none that were appealing. With each blind alley, at work and in his job search, he grew more anxious and panicky.

Finally, after about six months more, a job that he thought might work out was offered. He said to himself, "Look, it's not perfect, but I'm becoming desperate. The one good thing about the offer is that it gets me out of banking. Maybe after this new job, I can get into something I really want."

After sorting and shuffling paper at his new job for about three months, he knew he had made a bad mistake. The bank job suddenly looked like nirvana.

Tom D. made a negative career move—he left his current job because he convinced himself that it was no longer bearable, *not* for a better alternative. Many negative career moves are based on a distortion of and exaggerated reaction to one's situation—"Anything has to be better than what I'm currently doing"—and on a self-induced sense of desperation—"I will accept anything."

Desperation is a mixed blessing. On the positive side, it tells you that there is a serious problem with your current job, and that change is probably needed. On the negative side, it can obscure and distort your perceptions of the overall quality of both your current employment and alternative jobs.

Desperation is a powerful emotion. You feel helpless and out of control. It can make you grasp at straws—anything—to stop this all-pervasive sense of panic. As time passes and alternatives come and go, the emotion may intensify, and you become all too willing to grasp, not at straws, but at microscopically thin threads. This is, in essence, what happened to Tom D.—his desperation became so exacerbated after he turned down several job offers and opportunities that he accepted an inappropriate position.

The lesson to those facing a job-to-job move is one of self-discipline and self-control. Unless your current job is beyond salvage, wait until you can make a *positive* career move, a career move that will provide task interest and goal satisfaction. Following the example of Tom D. amounts to nothing more than precipitously seizing a short-term solution that provides momentary relief but which is doomed to fail.

People Tell Me That I Deserve Better

Your neighbor, who has a job as "assistant to God," continuously tells you to look for a position with more status, prestige, and money. Being a high school teacher, which you always found rewarding, suddenly doesn't seem as noble as it once did. You become dissatisfied to the point of going to a career counselor to determine the type of work most suitable to a person with your skills.

Your feelings of dissatisfaction cannot be blamed on this one individual. Everyday American life is the real culprit. Our culture holds the rich and famous in high esteem. We are constantly reminded by the popular press, television shows, and movies how much better, more interesting, more full of fun and intrigue, *other* people's lives are. Do you suppose that "Dallas," "Dynasty," and "Santa Barbara" would be popular if they featured the lives of *common* people?

When you begin to think about a job or even a career change primarily for reasons of status, prestige, and money, you increase your risk of becoming a career casualty. We could tell you *ad nauseam* of the wealthy and respected professionals who have told us that they hate what they are doing, that they selected a job or a career for the wrong reasons, and that they wish they could do it all over again.

Making a job or career change for someone else's reasons will be of very little benefit to you. Since it is *your* work and *your* life, the bases for your decisions must reflect *your* thinking, *your* interests, and *your* priorities.

It's *Their* Fault!

When events go badly, we tend to blame others for our self-made misfortunes. The reasons, of course, are not complex. By blaming others—or cursing our luck—for our problems at work, we avoid blaming ourselves or admitting that we are not as competent, masterful, or infallible as we thought or hoped. Our self-esteem and pride remain inviolate.

This pattern of thinking and behaving may be seen in the case of a disgruntled government manager we interviewed named Jeffrey D.

Jeffrey D. was a blamer and a complainer. As a mid-level administrator, he was forever grousing about the lack of resources to support his work.

It is true that local governments typically do not offer plush offices and individual secretaries for each manager, but Jeffrey D's working conditions, compared to people with similar jobs, were more than adequate. No other unit in local government had the support services that he had.

While he realized this, he was forever complaining about the limits of his resource support: Turn-around time on his projects took too long, staff was inadequate to help him with his demographic analyses, and he had to do too much of his own typing and filing.

He always found an inefficiency here, an inadequacy there, or a foul up somewhere else. Rarely did he look to himself as either a possible cause or solution for his problems.

He lacked a balanced perspective. He was unable to adjust to the constraints in the system and the imperfections in others; nor did he try to do his best with the status quo. No one complained nearly as much as he did, suggesting that others were able better to adjust to the same working conditions.

He was forever looking for a new job and announcing his displeasure with his coworkers.

Unfortunately, if *you* are a "blamer" and/or "complainer," transferring responsibility for your actions—or lack of action —to someone else, moving to another job will only serve to relocate the problem. "The fault, dear Brutus, is not in our stars, but in ourselves, that we are underlings."

The solution begins by taking responsibility for your mistakes and failures. You may wish to consider the following:

- Are your colleagues at work succeeding with a similar level of support?

- Have you honestly tried to make a go of it where you are? Have you thought, for instance, about ways to overcome work difficulties through creative solutions, innovative programs, and, of course, hard work?

- If your work difficulties are, indeed, the fault of another, have you discussed the matter with him or her and sought resolutions to the problems?

- Is there reason to believe that obstacles similar to the ones you are experiencing do not also exist at other firms?

If, after answering these questions, you conclude that you have done everything that you possibly can to remedy the situation, but that all your efforts have failed and that conditions would be better elsewhere, then a job-to-job transition begins to make sense. Be certain, however, that you really have given your current job your best shot.

I Give More Than I Receive

Another common mistake is that employees tend to over-value their contributions to a firm. This is not to say that some people are not underpaid, under appreciated, and only marginally respected. In many instances, however, individuals do not correctly evaluate their contributions or their pay back.

One reason for this is that workers may not realize what their companies are *really* paying for their efforts. As noted earlier, benefits are often taken for granted by employees; many fail to "add them in" to salary figures. The fact is that fringes—e.g., health insurance, paid vacation, workman's compensation—may constitute *as much as 40% of one's total compensation package.* Since employees do not see this as disposable income, they simply forget that it *is* a part of their remuneration. Even if individuals are aware of their fringe benefits, they may discount their actual dollar value.

Another reason for not feeling appreciated is a result of the different perspectives people hold in the workplace. When you complete a project for your company, you are intimately aware of every ounce of energy, effort, sweat, and tears that went into its success. More important, you *feel* it.

In contrast, your boss may at best have only an intellectual understanding of what you have achieved. He or she did not experience the personal trials and tribulations—the all nighters, working weekends, the endless worry—that went into your accomplishment.

Naturally, your contribution will mean more to you than to your boss. (Your boss, it may be comforting to remember, is going through the same experience with his or her boss.) Allow for the problem of different perspectives when you evaluate your current job situation, and realize that it is not necessary that a boss understand precisely the effort that you expended in completing a task. Recognition of the *quality* of your achievement is a more realistic expectation.

One final suggestion: To determine fully and accurately the fair market value of your services, consult data from the

Bureau of Labor Statistics and industry-wide salary surveys adjusted for geographical location. These data can give you a fairly good idea of how much your services are worth by industry, experience, job rank, and geographical region.

Then if you still believe you should seek employment elsewhere, at least your decision will be based on fact, not fancy.

I Just Can't Deal With The Ups And Downs

You have a disagreement with your boss. It happens to everyone. You want the firm to move to a computerized billing system, but your boss feels otherwise. "Too expensive," he tells you. "Besides, we have other priorities." In your heart of hearts you *know* he's wrong.

You give it one more try, but he won't budge. "We'll be in the dark ages forever," you are convinced. "I like my job and get along reasonably well with my boss, but at times like this I get so furious that I feel like marching into his office and throwing my resignation on his desk."

Resist this impulse. Not only is it foolish to make decisions when overwrought, but you are also ignoring the realities of the workplace. Work is like an elevator, filled with ups and downs (although it is the "jerks" that probably bother us most). A certain degree of frustration is built into the life of an active, talented person. Remove yourself from the anger of the moment. Reflect on past accomplishments. Project yourself forward to future successes. Evaluating your job based solely on what is happening *at the moment* often leads to distorted perceptions of reality.

Before making *any* job-to-job transition, be certain that your personal career ledger—your emotional balance sheet— is reviewed in its totality. Factor in *all* the good and *all* the bad, not a single moment or event.

You can only draw an accurate picture of your current and prospective jobs if you use all the hues and colors that comprise the palette of your work experience.

Nine

Changing Jobs For The *Right* Reasons

When The Grass *Is* Greener

We have discussed the wrong reasons for staying at a job and the wrong reasons for leaving. In most cases, fears and rationalizations either prevent an individual from making a transition that is timely or thrust a person into a transition that he or she is not ready to make. But knowing the *wrong* reasons doesn't tell you what the *right* reasons are for changing jobs.

It is not feasible—perhaps not even possible—to discuss the myriad of circumstances that may convince you to look for another job. We wish, instead, to offer several general guidelines which pertain to many situations.

It makes sense to leave a job if you are simply not succeeding at it.

If you are not fulfilling the major requirements of your job and failing to achieve what your firm expects of you, you should seriously consider changing jobs. It is important to be fair to yourself and give yourself sufficient time both to learn your job well and to evaluate your performance. If, however, six months or a year after learning the subtleties of your work, you find that you are still failing to meet your firm's expectations as well as your own, there is sufficient cause to believe that you and your job or you and your firm have been mismatched.

The longer you stay at such a job, the more difficult it may become to find a new position. A weak track record over an extended period of time may make you as popular as last year's teen idol. There is, furthermore, an increased likelihood that you will be fired, which would make securing another job especially difficult.

A pattern of failure often results in frustration, emotional stress, low self-esteem, and a pervasive feeling of helplessness. For professional as well as personal reasons, then, if you are unsuccessful and you cannot turn it around, you should make a concerted effort to find a new job, one at which you can win—or at least learn the skills you need to be a winner later.

It makes sense to leave a job, although you are currently succeeding, if you believe the firm can offer you no new challenges.

Even success can become boring. If there are no new challenges and little variety in your work, it may be difficult to maintain a high level of interest and motivation. When these conditions are present, it is time to consider making a job-to-job transition.

This is, we should add, an excellent vantage point from which to leave a firm. You have established yourself as a successful employee and should not find it difficult to locate a job with more challenges and greater upward mobility. Some might argue that you should leave well enough alone, that as long as you are succeeding there is no point in leaving. But consider the possibility that you are not being fair to yourself by remaining in such a situation. There is no telling what you will be able to achieve, what heights you will be able to reach, in a more challenging and expansive setting.

It makes sense to leave a job if you believe you have reached the maximum level of advancement that the firm has to offer.

There are numerous reasons that may lead an individual to conclude that he or she has reached the saturation point in a firm. The "Hula-Hoop" phenomenon, for instance, may be operative: A firm may have had a fabulously successful product or a high-profit year, but then fall back into a rut of unimaginative activities and low earnings, which seem to be a truer reflection of the firm's quality. Without growth, the firm, you may conclude, will not be able to offer you advancement in the foreseeable future.

Another cause for believing that you will stagnate is the promotion policy of a firm. You may observe, for instance, that those promoted to top management positions are always individuals with technical training or work experience widely different from yours (e.g., only individuals with a strong science background are promoted to top levels, while your strengths lie in sales). If these or similar conditions are present, you should probably look for employment elsewhere.

You may tend to hope that promotion practices will change, that you will, for instance, be the first person from sales to reach the top. Companies, like people, have personalities, and those personalities often doggedly resist change. If you wish to wait for a change in promotion practices, just realize that it may take a while...a lifetime or two.

It makes sense to leave a job if you have never found it interesting and don't expect it to become more interesting in the future.

It is, of course, a mistake to accept such a job in the first place, although you, especially at the beginning of a career, are not always the arbiter of your own destiny. The "task interest" rule we discussed in the first chapter suggests the folly of remaining in this situation. The interest you have in a job is one of the major determinants of your current and future success. Without the requisite interest, you may find that the quality of your work will decline and continue in an an ever-widening downward spiral.

It makes sense to leave a job in which you were once interested, but in which your interest has decreased to the point that you would need a microscope to locate it.

Neither jobs nor employees remain static. While your initial decision to accept this job may have been sound, it is certainly possible that either you or the job or both have changed over time. Your interest in and commitment to your work must be frequently reappraised. If you find that your interest has declined dramatically and that the future seems to hold little promise of reigniting your enthusiasm, it is time to look elsewhere.

It is time to leave a job if you no longer feel happy.

Certainly no one should remain unhappy, and if the cause is your job, leave as soon as you can. The problem is that unhappiness has many parents: An unpleasant family life may make you feel unhappy at work; your unhappiness may reside deep within your psyche; or your difficulty may, indeed, be work related.

Before deciding to leave a job, determine the exact nature and cause of your discontent. If you believe you need assistance in making this determination, seek help from a psychologist, psychiatrist, or counselor. This will prevent you from leaving a job when it may not be related to your woes.

If unhappiness comes from within, then no job, no location, and no group of friends will be able to make one happy. "The mind," wrote John Milton, "is in its own place, and in itself can make a Heav'n of Hell, or a Hell of Heav'n."

You may, of course, conclude, after thoroughly analyzing yourself and your job, that your unhappiness is, indeed, work related. It may be that your firm or industry is not as socially responsive as you would like; that the objectives, goals, and policies of your firm are not acceptable to you; that the basic limitations of your work or your firm bother you; or that your work environment is unpleasant.

You may also disagree ethically or morally with your boss or your company. An auto mechanic told us, "I left because they were padding customer's bills." A physician reported that she left the medical group with which she was associated because "they were unethical in dealing with their patients." In such cases, a job-to-job transition may be the only way to restore your sense of well-being.

Looking Into The Future: Commitment And Potential

One of the greatest difficulties in implementing these guidelines is that if you are like the rest of us mere mortals, you are not blessed (or cursed) with clairvoyance. While you may not be able to determine with precision what the future at your present job holds for you, you may receive some indication by talking with your boss. He or she should be able to tell you how committed the firm is to helping you to grow as a professional, to maintaining your interest, to achieving your goals.

The key is *commitment*. If your firm has little vested interest in your future, then the choice of what to do becomes substantially clearer.

Commitment on the part of your firm may take many forms. Is management interested in promoting you? Are they anxious to give you assignments of increasing importance? Will they extend your sphere of job responsibility? Will they increasingly seek your input on major decisions? Are they planning to have you attend management development programs?

You also may wish to judge if other employees at your level in the firm are being shown more corporate commitment than you are. One caveat, however: Comparisons, as we noted earlier, are difficult and dangerous to make, for no one in the firm is exactly like you.

It is also easy to misread the signals that management gives. You may, for example, see a coworker receiving seemingly better treatment than you, but the reason may be that he or she needs more training and remedial work. It may also be that his or her boss is inadequate, and management is supporting your coworker so that the unit will not collapse. Again, the most accurate comparison is with yourself.

Looking into the future also requires that you assess what your firm can do for you. Some businesses are so small that they present limited opportunities for upward movement. Even though they may be committed to you, they will have little to offer in terms of professional growth and development. Individuals in the allied medical professions, for instance, may face this problem because there are so few hierarchical levels within one institution. Typically, they must look outside of their organizations for promotion.

Part of looking into the future is to assess the economic viability of your unit and/or firm. Fiscal problems often result in reorganizing a unit, shifting personnel, and hiring and firing managers. It is a withering cross fire in which to be caught.

The decision to leave a firm or to stay is complex and should not be made in a vacuum. Analyze carefully and methodically your career pattern up to the present, the value indicators of your performance, the firm's future commitment to you, and your sense of personal and professional growth, development, and interest. Decisions of this nature are never easy, and there is never a guarantee that you are making the proper choice. The best you can hope for is to make an informed decision based on as much data as you can amass.

Most important, do not fear making a transition. Confront the future and engage it with the same optimism and assurance as Alfred Lord Tennyson's Ulysses, who, after completing his travels, resolved in the future "to strive, to seek, to find, and not to yield."

Moving To Greener Pastures

You have made the hard decision: You are going to look for another job. You are now in a period of flux and tentativeness. You feel like Janus, the Roman god with two faces looking in opposite directions. The difficulty and ambivalence of your present situation is understandable. Here are several guidelines for helping you complete the job-to-job transition successfully.

If at all possible, stay at your old job until you secure a new one.

It is much more difficult to make a career move when you're unemployed. Prospective employers will wonder *why* you are not currently working and may well assume that you were fired or asked to resign. Not only does this make getting a job more problematical, but it also may reduce your ability to negotiate the best possible salary and working conditions. Furthermore, the absence of a steady income may put pressure on you to accept a less-than-desirable job.

As badly as you want to leave your current job, don't allow the quality of your work to suffer.

The desire to change jobs is never a valid reason for failing to take pride in yourself and in your work. Moreover, if a prospective employer learns that you are not a high performer, it may affect his or her desire to woo you away.

Repackaging Yourself

It is time to update your resume. We recommend keeping a Career Development File (CDF) during your entire professional life—a manila folder in which you keep documentation of your job-related achievements and accomplishments. Items that may be included in a CDF:

- Samples of your writing: reports, feasibility studies, position papers;
- Notifications of performance bonuses;
- Notifications of merit raises;
- Notifications of promotions;
- Letters of commendation from your employer;
- Letters of appreciation from clients and customers;
- Memos citing how much money you made for or saved your employer;
- Certificates of additional training and areas of competency;
- Copies of your performance appraisals;
- Memos or letters citing your role in successful projects.

This information may now be used to update your resume. It will also be invaluable material as you progress throughout your career.

Get The Word Out

Having been employed for a year or more gives you at least one major advantage over a recent high school or college graduate. You have begun to establish a network of business associates: vendors, clients, customers, colleagues, even competitors. These are individuals who may very likely give you your next job lead, if not the job itself.

According to Richard Bolles, author of the job-hunting classic, <u>What Color Is Your Parachute?</u>, only 20% of all jobs are found through the traditional approaches of scouring the classified pages, responding to advertisements, and sending out "blind" cover letters with resumes attached. Which means that *80%* of all jobs are filled through the non-systematic methods of following word-of-mouth leads and relying on professional and social acquaintances. The message is clear: Your network is your best employment agency.

Recently we met an attorney working as a junior associate for an excellent New York City firm. In his second year out of law school, he was grossing $60,000 a year. He was assigned to a client who was the chief executive officer and president of a large construction company. The CEO was so pleased with the quality of the young man's work that he made him an appealing offer: "Come work for me full-time as my in-house legal counsel, and I'll pay you $250,000 per year. Does that sound okay?"

After probably whispering to himself, "Be still, my heart," the junior associate quietly uttered, "When do I start?"

While your salary may be different, the theme is the same: Your network will most likely be your ticket to the next stop in your career travels. Set your network in action by simply informing those who comprise it that you are back on the job market. This can be done through a variety of mediums— lunch dates, letters, telephone calls, casual conversations.

A difficult decision must now be made: Should you apprise your current employer that you are on the job market, or should you keep it *sub rosa?* One high-profile chief executive officer is said to have valued, if not demanded, the complete loyalty of his employees. He even "surgically removed" the names of employees from plaques and awards if they had the temerity to move to other firms.

If your boss or the culture of your firm values loyalty to that degree, keep your job search "top secret." If you are unsure of the reaction of your boss and colleagues, play it safe and keep the matter private. In any event, the fear of top management finding out should not, as we have advised in the last chapter, deter you from investigating or making a job change.

On The Road Again

If you have used your network and created a resume that does not make you appear as flotsam and jetsam, you will probably be asked to several interviews. As with your transition from high school or college to the corporate world, this face-to-face exchange with your potential employer could have enormous consequences.

Let us imagine a scenario in which Carl Ego, a young, ambitious executive who believes that he is the greatest thing to happen to the business world since the invention of money, goes to an interview with a potential new employer.

Interviewer: "Why are you leaving Bosses, Executives, and Lowlife Clearing House (BELCH)?"

Carl Ego: "That's a fair question. There are several reasons why I'm leaving BELCH: I've exceeded their expectations and grown out of the job. I wish to undertake something more challenging and rewarding. At the risk of sounding overconfident, I was ready from the very beginning for more than they were equipped to give me. That's why I'm here."

Interviewer: "What are your salary requirements?"

Carl Ego: "Well, I feel I earned my stripes in the year I've spent at BELCH. I believe that I now deserve between $100,000 and $120,000. I would also expect use of a company car as part of my TCP— you know, total compensation package. Naturally, I don't like to focus on the negative, but if things don't work out, I would like to have a nine-month severance pay clause included in my employment contract."

Interviewer: "Let me backtrack for a moment. Are there any other reasons why you are leaving BELCH?"

Carl Ego: "Now that you mention it, yes. I don't want to tell tales out of school, but my former employers had a terribly narrow view of what it means to develop new and innovative products. Typically, they would observe how a competitor's new product line was doing, and if the market seemed responsive, they would copy it rather than taking a leadership role in product design."

"Pride," according to the Bible, "goeth before the fall."

Flushed with the success of his first job experience and euphoric over the fact that several firms desired him, our young corporate champion believes and acts as though he can manage the solar system. He approaches his interviewer with a degree of confidence that borders on unmitigated arrogance. He makes ludicrous salary demands, topped off with a request for a golden parachute that experienced executives ten years his senior would be lucky to get. In his orgy of egotism, he attacks the integrity, as well as the intelligence, of his former firm and its CEO.

What he failed to realize is that humility and honest self-appraisal would be much better received by an interviewer than pretension and self-aggrandizement.

Since making your first transition, you have had the opportunity to assess what you do well and what needs to be improved. Communicate this to the interviewer. Make it clear that you believe you have much to offer but that you also feel that you have much to learn. Describe your accomplishments without disparaging the work of others. If your record is solid, there is no need to "gild the lily." Interviewers can be shrewd judges of character, ability, and personality. Coming on like a midway barker at a county fair may very well be seen by him or her as a disguise for feelings of inadequacy and insecurity.

Lateral Moves: Yes or No?

The value of a lateral move is a hotly contested issue. One must, before deciding if a lateral move will be beneficial, define precisely what he or she wishes to accomplish professionally in the short and long term.

A lateral move may well be useful at this point in your career. It may, for instance, expand your experience base or allow you to acquire additional skills. Sales experience can be complemented by a new job that will provide experience in marketing or merchandising. A staff planning specialist who acquires line experience can increase his or her chances of landing a management job in the years ahead.

Perhaps the job you are considering, although not very different from the one you currently have, is with a company that will offer more mobility in the future. Maybe the job is *identical* to the one you now have, but your new boss has an industry-wide reputation for providing excellent training for executives on the rise.

A lateral move, then, can make a great deal of sense if you view it as an investment in your career education. Just hope that the experience is worth the tuition. We do not recommend a lateral move undertaken primarily for a change of geographical scenery or in the unrealistic hope that something will "break your way" at a new firm.

Saying Goodbye

Even though you may feel that you would rather have daily root canal than stay at your current job, the urge to give a "high-five" handshake to everyone should be suppressed. Be gracious, diplomatic, and professional in your departure. Reputations and labels from the past have an uncanny way of sticking to people.

Explain to your soon-to-be former boss the bases of your decision without bad-mouthing your past experience. You have undoubtedly gained valuable skills from the firm you are leaving; if so, do not be reluctant to mention and express appreciation for this. Naturally, you should give sufficient notice of your departure, usually a minimum of two weeks.

Your job-to-job transition means someone else's move as well. Be sensitive to this. Take whatever steps you think are necessary to help your replacement make a smooth transition into your former position. By doing so you will be more likely to keep your former firm and its executives as part of your professional network.

How you relate news of your departure to your peers and subordinates is crucial. They will undoubtedly want to know your reasons for leaving. A supercilious pose or a patronizing attitude is not only rude, it will also cause resentment that will not soon be forgotten. Share the thinking that went into your decision to leave, diplomatically and sensitively.

A seemingly small act which has, in reality, major career implications is to take the contents of your rolodex, phone and address cards, date book, and similar types of information with you; just make certain it *is* yours. People with whom you have worked, people who know and respect and enjoy you, will be valuable members of your professional network in the future. Note, however, that taking company documents could give rise to legal problems. It is advisable to check first.

A Rookie Again

Job and career transitions are a new beginning. On the positive side are the opportunities to face different challenges, meet new people, and explore new surroundings. On the negative side are the anxieties and uncertainties, the frustration of unlearning old ways of viewing the corporate world and acquiring new ways of thinking and behaving. It is not, of course, the first time this has happened to you. You now know how to go about learning the rules, the norms, the culture of a firm.

You may initially experience a discomforting tension within yourself between your awareness of your abilities and talents and your unawareness of the basic facts of life at your new firm. In this sense, a new beginning means going back three giant steps and again becoming a corporate rookie.

There is another sense in which you are a rookie. You have come to a new firm with no laurels upon which to rest, for your accomplishments were made in another world, at another time, in another context—virtually in another dimension. Your boss will want to know, "What can you do for me now?" and he or she does mean *"now."* As one engineer told us, "When I was interviewed, really courted, they couldn't stop talking about my achievements. When I showed up for the new job, it was like I had no history at all; the slate was wiped clean. I felt that I needed to hit a home run—and fast."

This is, then, a new kind of rookie experience. In your first career change—from campus to corporation—you were probably given an extended honeymoon, an adjustment period, a protracted amnesty for mistakes. In this transition, the expectation is that you know how to do the job—you are a rookie with experience.

It is not uncommon for these new demands and expectations to cause a mixture of transitional nostalgia and transitional fear, the former being caused by the latter. These feelings are predictable and respectable; they are inextricably linked to virtually all transitions. The nostalgia will quickly fade, and the fear will be transformed into excitement and enthusiasm. The very issues that aroused your fear and anxiety will now be seen as challenges and opportunities and will be attacked with all the zeal and fervor of a new convert.

When the negative side of any career change is understood and faced, the positive side has the opportunity to flourish.

Ten

BEING FIRED AND BEING PROMOTED

Work, like true love, rarely runs on a smooth course. Just as you are settling into a comfortable working schedule, establishing a network of friends at the firm, and paying off your student loans, the axe falls. You've been FIRED!

The reasons for losing a job are many, and often they are beyond your control. We do not, however, want to dwell on the negative aspects of what has happened—you have become, unfortunately, quite knowledgeable in that area. Rather, let's discuss how to put your working life back into order.

Life In The Valley

Step 1: Recognize that the world has not ended.

It is hard to console someone who has recently lost his or her job, but do keep events in perspective. You are an educated, talented individual with much to offer to the workplace. What has happened should be seen as nothing more than a momentary setback. Few people enjoy careers without some detours or potholes along the way; it goes with the territory. Give yourself a day or two to kick the garbage can and curse the gods. Then start to prepare for your next job.

Step 2: Do not burn your bridges.

The worst mistakes people make when they lose their jobs often occur within the first 72 hours after they are terminated. We realize the sense of hurt, even betrayal, that you are experiencing, but the way to put your career back on track is *not* to lash out at your former employer. You may find that he or she can offer valuable assistance in finding a new job. Let your head, not your emotions, dictate your conduct.

Step 3: Negotiate a severance package.

When you are fired, asked to resign, or laid off, discuss with your employer what type of severance package is being offered. Be sure to inquire about the continuation of insurance programs, especially health and disability insurance.

Out-placement packages are negotiable, so you do not have to immediately accept what is offered. If you had any type of contract with the firm, consult a labor attorney if you need counsel. Even though it may sound awkward at this time, discuss with your former employer if he or she is willing to write a reference letter for you.

Step 4: Take job search information with you.

Part of an effective job search is rooted in comprehensive lists of potential employers or employment leads. Ask for permission to take with you the names of people with whom you had contact while an employee, names that appear, for instance, on your rolodex or in a company telephone directory.

Step 5: Determine why it happened.

Often the reason for losing a job is beyond your control— "the result of business necessity" is the phrase employers frequently use when terminating someone. Yet the possibility that you bore some of the responsibility for losing your job should not be ignored.

After your emotions have subsided and you can think clearly, look within yourself and reflect on your workplace experiences. Was the person-job fit wrong? Did your job, for instance, demand a high-pressure, "never say die" sales approach, while you preferred a laid-back, "let the product sell itself" style?

Instead of trying to work with a difficult boss, did you simply assume that it was not worth the effort? Did you always keep lines of communication with your boss open? Did you establish a pattern of tardiness: missing deadlines, being late for meetings, asking for extensions on completing projects, holding up the work of coworkers, keeping clients waiting? Were your interpersonal skills found wanting? Did you interact congenially and professionally with your boss, coworkers, and clients?

Past behavior is often a reliable predictor of future behavior. If you believe that you were partly to blame for your termination, this is an excellent time to examine and correct those faults. Read about how to manage a difficult boss. Take a course on time management. Enroll in a seminar for improving human relations skills.

Step 6: Start job searching as soon as possible.

There is often a tendency for people who have lost their jobs to withdraw into themselves and lick their wounds. This is counterproductive behavior; instead, strike out with renewed vigor and enthusiasm to find another, even better, job.

Start your new job search by calling on your network of friends and associates. Telephone or make lunch dates with people you met while working in your former job to discuss job opportunities. One of the advantages you have now, as opposed to when you were looking for your *first* job, is that you have built up a network of contacts that may help you get back into the work force. Respond to want ads in newspapers and trade journals, but remember that 80% of jobs come from personal contacts.

Since you will have to update your resume and hone your interviewing skills, review chapters two and three of this book.

Step 7: Prepare a good answer for: "Why did you leave your last job?"

If the reason you lost your last job was "the result of business necessity," responding to this question is not difficult, for it does not necessarily reflect on the quality of your work.

If, however, you lost your job because of poor performance, acknowledge it. Explain why you believe your past job did not work out. Objectively discuss the mistakes that you think you made, as well as any mistakes that were made by others. In your answer be sure to focus on several issues which will put your candidacy in a positive light:

- What you have learned from the experience;
- How you should have better handled matters;
- Why you think the problem(s) will not reoccur;
- What actions you have taken to overcome any deficiencies that may have created the problem in your last job.

Step 8: Don't make the same mistake(s) twice.

If you lost your job because of a poor person-job fit, the job was not what you thought it would be, or you misread the culture and management style of the firm, learn from these mistakes so that you don't make them a second time.

Making a good choice also means not grasping at straws. You are under pressure, but it is better to take a short-term or part-time job rather than accept a job that violates the Success Equation discussed in chapter 1. Be confident that the right job will eventually come along.

Step 9: Use your support network.

It is important to use your support group of family and friends for emotional reassurance—that is what support groups are for. Heavy loads are often borne more easily when they are shared.

Continue those aspects of your life that give you pleasure —sports, hobbies, and reading—activities which willhelp you maintain a sense of equilibrium during your job search.

Step 10: Maintain your self-esteem.

There are few experiences quite as ego deflating as losing a job. For the young career traveler filled with dreams and aspirations the decompression from the burst balloon can be very painful. You may begin to question your abilities, self-worth, and self-efficacy.

While these feelings are predictable, balance them with the conviction that you are an educated, talented, and worthwhile individual who happened to get into a situation that simply did not work out. You still possess the skills, abilities, and initiative that a future employer will value. Life goes on, often for the better.

It should come as no surprise that many people who have been fired note that it was the best thing that ever happened to them and their careers.

Life On The Mountain Top

Mountain tops are a lot better than valleys, yet there may be just as many obstacles. What happens if, instead of going down, you're heading up, to the heady ranks of management?

Successfully making the transition from non-manager to manager begins with learning a new way of thinking. Your "mind set"—the way you are predisposed to approach issues and problems in the workplace—must change dramatically. We suggest that you examine the following four mind-sets and try to incorporate them into your thinking and behavior.

1) Think Of Yourself As A Facilitator

Great managers are great facilitators. You must think of yourself not simply as a "doer," but as a "path clearer," as one who removes the piles of organizational, environmental, and economic debris to allow both you and your subordinates to march directly to your objectives.

There are numerous dimensions to being a facilitator. If your employees are short on resources, it is your job to secure them or to devise a way of making existing resources stretch further. If subordinates are confused on a project, you must listen to their problems and resolve their confusion. If other departments are not cooperating with yours, you must create the coordination that is needed. If there are personnel problems in your unit that are impeding progress, it is up to you to overcome them so that the unit may function productively. In a nutshell, being a manager means solving problems, often other peoples' problems.

There are several guidelines that should help you be a successful facilitator:

Listen more; talk less.

In order to help your employees solve problems, you will have to thoroughly understand the difficulties they are facing, which necessitates listening and answering questions rather than commanding or demanding.

As a subordinate you actually worked for fewer people than you do as a manager—now you have to work with all your subordinates. The first step in doing this is to listen to their problems, questions, feedback, and suggestions. Consider your employees as working *with* you, not *for* you.

Be accessible.

Be available to your employees when they need you. Management involves walking around the unit and asking questions such as, "How's it going?;" "Do you want me to give you a hand with this project?;" "What can I do to help?"

Asking these questions is an open invitation for your employees to use you as a facilitator. We have heard too often of managers who stay comfortably locked in the womb of their own offices. Until they're fired for being lousy managers.

Make no false promises.

While it is crucial for a new manager to ask, "What can I do to help?," offering to help and then failing to provide it is more harmful than not making the offer in the first place, for it will cost you your credibility. The next time you ask an employee that question, he or she will know that you are just playing a verbal game and won't take your offer seriously.

Making false promises is sometimes the result of naivete. A new manager, flushed with a sense of recently acquired power and authority, may make outrageous promises to his or her staff—pay adjustments, promotions, additional resources—promises he or she would like to keep but does not yet realize he or she cannot.

Make a realistic appraisal of what you can and can't accomplish. While your new position may bring you more authority than you possessed before, it is probably *less* authority than you had hoped for or thought it would be. Honest recognition of one's limitations will command as much respect from subordinates as problem-solving initiatives.

2) You Can't Do It All By Yourself

Independence and individuality are two of the hallmarks of a successful non-manager. As an employee, you relied largely on yourself to get the job done: follow-up, follow-through, running the copy machine, collating, making phone calls, flagging down leads—you name it, you did it.

One of the most difficult lessons a new manager has to learn is to delegate work and responsibility. In a very real sense, it requires you to *un*learn the behaviors and attitudes you had as a subordinate and learn new ones. Being able to delegate work and responsibility demands that the new manager replace the notion, "If it is going to be done right, I have to do it myself," with faith in the willingness, ability, and resourcefulness of others.

3) Employ *Several* Styles Of Management

A manager will often find him- or herself in charge of a pluralistic group of employees with widely varying personalities, dispositions, and attitudes. He or she will also be confronted with a rapidly changing, fluid, and flexible workplace—unique situations, new problems, unusual issues, and odd circumstances have increasingly become the rule rather than the exception. Given the diversity of people and situations a manager must deal with, it should follow that he or she must be able to employ a variety of management styles.

There is no *one* best way to manage; there are multiple ways. The objective is to match a particular management style to each specific situation and employee. If an employee is confused over how to solve a problem or reach a goal, a direct, interventionist leadership style would probably be the most effective. If you have a new employee who is feeling frightened and insecure, a more supportive leadership style may be called for. If you have experienced, self-motivated employees, you may wish to use a participatory managerial style, in which you solicit their recommendations before making a decision.

Explaining to your employees that you intend to use a variety of leadership styles will help them understand that they are not working for a chameleon. Whenever possible, explain to them the logic—the "why"—of your actions. Contrary to popular belief, why you do what you do *is* their business.

There is a variety of methods you can employ to develop managerial styles in which you feel deficient.

Formal seminars and workshops are readily available. If, for instance, you feel uncomfortable with directive- or goal-oriented styles of leadership, you may wish to attend an assertiveness development workshop or a goal-setting program, respectively.

Observing managers who possess leadership styles you wish to develop can be extremely beneficial. Listening to how managers coach their employees, deliver bad news, reinforce outstanding performance, and seek information for decisions can be of direct assistance to you.

You may also wish to identify a role model in your organization and ask him or her for guidance.

"Mind playing," which involves "picturing yourself" successfully using management styles which are new for you, is one of the easiest and most convenient methods for overcoming the psychological obstacles preventing you from developing diverse styles.

Role playing a specific management style with a spouse, friend, or colleague is an effective approach for developing new managerial styles. If you have difficulty, for instance, confronting an angry employee, and confrontation is the appropriate managerial style, role play a scene between you and the irate subordinate.

4) Think of Yourself As A Boss *And* A Friend

It is important to have friends at work, for they can provide you with valuable guidance and support. A promotion to a supervisory level does not mean that you must give up friendships with your former peers. As a new manager, however, your friendships with subordinates must never result in preferential treatment or even the *appearance* of favoritism. Equity, as well as the perception of equity, must be maintained at all times. This means that at staff meetings you must elicit the opinions of those people you dislike as well as those you like. The criteria for promotions, bonuses, and pay raises must also be performance-related, not based on friendship.

You must never allow friendship to interfere with work performance. If your friend is doing a dreadful job, you must communicate this to him or her. Doing so does not mean that you cannot be that person's friend; in fact, the friendship itself may be the catalyst for his or her improvement. If your friend develops ill feelings toward you for negative sanctions, he or she may not be a friend worth having.

A related problem sometimes occurs when a young manager is placed in charge of an older employee. If you sense resentment because of your youth, give the older employee time to observe your abilities as a manager. Time may solve the problem.

If the resentment continues, however, then it is probably best to confront it directly. Your meeting with the disgruntled employee should not be adversarial. Explain that you feel that he or she seems uncomfortable working with you, and that you would like to know if you are in any way responsible. Potentially accepting some of the responsibility for the problem should create a positive climate for problem solving; blaming, threatening, and reprimanding will only harden the problem.

You may also wish to discuss the value of teamwork in a unit, that no one wins if there is a morale problem and a lack of support. If the older employee still cannot accept your role as manager, then the problem is with him or her and not with you. Discuss with that individual the feasibility of transferring to another unit or leaving the firm.

Implicit in our discussion of the various mind sets for a new manager is the notion that being a good manager means working well with people. A good manager talks to employees with respect, not impatience; asks them questions to seek information, not to figure out who to blame; treats them with dignity, not indifference; offers kindness, not frustration; and points out weaknesses with sensitivity, not abrasiveness.

We have dwelled on the difficulties more than the joys of being a new manager. So that you do not curse your fate for being promoted, let us end on a positive note.

You have been elevated to a position which will not only command a greater salary but which will also allow you to grow professionally and personally.

You will acquire a full range of organizational and managerial skills.

You will develop a more global understanding of your firm.

You will become familiar with other administrative and support units and how they function together.

You will interact with offices and people with whom you formerly had little, if any, contact.

And you will develop greater creativity and imagination as you attempt to solve problems and work with subordinates.

You will become a mentor, a father confessor, a marriage counselor, an arbitrator, and a psychologist.

In resolving problems and conflicts, you will develop and sensitize parts of yourself that were dormant.

You will suddenly become, despite your age or wishes, a role model and have to bear the responsibilities attendant upon such a position.

And as you grow and develop and learn, you will have the rich satisfaction of helping others to grow and develop and learn.

Samuel Johnson defined happiness, not as a fixed state, but as a process, a pursuit, a constantly changing condition in which one is given new challenges: "Do not suffer life to stagnate," he wrote, "it will grow muddy for want of motion: commit yourself again to the current of the world."

As a new manager, that is precisely what you are doing.

Eleven

WORKING SINGLE TO WORKING MARRIED

Despite the fact that approximately one-half of all marriages in the United States end in separation or divorce, marriage is not in danger of becoming obsolete. Americans tied the knot in the frenetic 1980s at a rate similar to that of the more tranquil '50s.

This is not attributable to a naive optimism or wishful thinking, but rather to the continuing realization that two people can achieve fulfillment and happiness by sharing their lives. Although individuals are marrying at an older age than they were three decades ago, if you are a "working single," it is likely that you will eventually become a "working married," and it is likely to happen early in your career.

The work-related issues involved in this transition are often overlooked, and for entirely understandable reasons. Work is prosaic and pedestrian compared to the rapturous world of love and romance. When one is in love, he or she does not want to hear about how marriage is going to impact one's job and career. Yet the reality is that work and marriage have a profound and complex effect on one another.

As with all transitions, the extent to which you understand and prepare for these complexities will determine whether you will be in control of events or whether they will control you. We realize that each person's and each couple's transition from working single to working married has elements, nuances, and dimensions that are unique, and that the relationship between work and marriage does not lend itself to a brief or facile analysis. We believe, however, that there are several fundamental problems or issues in making this transition which are common to most couples. It is these problems that we wish to discuss.

My Work Time Is No Longer Exclusively *My* Time

Despite anguished cries of "my time is not my own," single working individuals possess a relatively high degree of freedom and flexibility in determining how they spend their work-related time compared to their married counterparts. Perhaps you have experienced one of the following scenarios:

> *Scenario #1:* As an unmarried student you were a night owl, preferring to do your most difficult work in the solitary calm of the late night. That predilection has persisted—you still prefer to work while others are preparing for bed. Being a workaholic, you frequently spend the hours from 10:00 P.M. to 1:00 A.M., as well as weekend afternoons, doing extra projects for your boss.
>
> For long stretches at a time, you live on cigarettes, coffee, and will power. You are relieved that you alone can determine when you do the work that you take home, and that you do not have to answer to anyone for the extended hours you keep.

Scenario # 2: It is the norm, you have found, for junior associates in your law firm to work at least 60 hours a week in order to bill their clients for the expected 35 hours a week. Your work schedule, therefore, usually ends at 8:00 and includes most Saturdays.

Furthermore, you are acutely aware that the senior partners enjoy seeing their young associates burying their noses in case studies in the firm's law library (little wonder that all the senior partners have flat noses). If you have any hope of someday becoming a partner, you realize that this work ethic must be continued.

Scenario # 3: As a young salesperson four years on the job, you accept the fact that you must do a great deal of traveling. Sometimes you are on the road three or four days a week, have to fly Sunday to attend an early Monday morning meeting, or don't make it home until Saturday afternoon after a late Friday afternoon call.

This schedule presents no problems for you because you can come and go as you please. It's your time and your company's time; no one else is demanding a portion of it.

Scenario #4: Last-minute or spur-of-the-moment work has become commonplace in your life as the assistant manager of the men's sportswear department in a large retail store. Your day was going smoothly until management, after receiving the latest computer print-out of sales, decides at 4:00 on Friday to hold a sale in your department—starting Saturday at 9:00.

This will demand at least another five hours of work, but since you had nothing planned for the evening anyway, you accept the task philosophically. After an injection of caffeine, you begin the arduous task of recalculating prices, retagging items, and designing and displaying appropriate graphics. That's retail!

These scenarios have one common element. They all demand a rare and precious commodity: *flexible time*. To the extent that your time is your own—that you can make decisions independently about how to spend it—you will be able to meet a variety of work-related demands with a minimum of disruption to your private life.

As soon as another person enters your life, however, the effects of your decisions on that individual become a crucial element in determining how your time is spent. Your previous commitment to yourself and to your firm has now been expanded—from this point on virtually all work-related activities that demand additional hours or an unusual schedule will have an impact on the personal and private lives of both you *and* your spouse.

Fulfillment of the emotional, intellectual, and physical needs of each party is basic to a successful marriage. For this to be achieved, individuals must spend a sufficient amount of quality time together—"our time" as opposed to "my time."

Probably the greatest single barrier to sharing experiences and sharing time is the demands that our careers make upon us. A variation of the traditional "eternal triangle" occurs, with a job competing with a spouse for attention. When this happens, complaints may replace the above scenarios:

> Complaint # 1: *"We generally only have time to wave to one another. I'm out of the house by 7:00, which is when he is just getting up. I get home at 5:30, but he doesn't arrive until after 8:00, and then he is too exhausted and drained for anything more than a perfunctory hello and a kiss on the cheek.*

> Complaint # 2: *"We both travel; it's a part of our jobs. If it were not for Ma Bell, we would have no relationship at all. When I got married I imagined having candlelit dinners, not pouring my heart out to a telephone receiver."*

Complaint # 3: *"Sometimes I think she cares more about her job than she does about me. When her boss calls, she jumps and puts everything on hold, including me. She spends an hour on the phone talking to him about business problems, but when I want to talk to her about problems that I'm having at the office, she just says, 'Don't worry, honey, it'll work out.'"*

Complaint # 4: *"We live in separate worlds. We never have the time to share experiences; we simply keep drifting further apart. We're more like business partners than lovers."*

Complaint # 5: *"I need to work at the office until 8:00. It's not by choice; it's by demand. My wife resents that I'm not around when she needs me. I can understand this, but I have a job to do. What's worse, my work has started to become sloppy because I feel obligated to rush home. I just can't seem to win."*

Assigning responsibility or ascribing blame in these situations is impossible. More importantly, it is unproductive and harmful. There are no villains or victims, heroes or goats, only people who are experiencing the difficulties, frustrations, and confusion of managing both their professional and personal lives. Time, or more specifically the lack of time, is at the basis of these problems. Since spending sufficient time together is a vital element in maintaining a successful marital relationship, we wish to suggest several methods of resolving time conflicts.

Creating A Marital Time Map

Review each other's work/date book for the past several months. This should provide you with a sense of what a typical working week and month is like. Patterns should emerge. Many businesspeople attend key meetings at regularly scheduled times each week, travel on specific days of the week or month, and experience cyclical periods of intense work and slack time.

After you have recorded these patterns, list the activities that you both enjoy doing together—theater, movies, travel, dining out, taking walks, reading the Sunday morning paper in bed. Then match the activities with the open periods of your work schedules.

This process should be repeated on a monthly basis, so that your marital time map will not only be based on past experience but also on what you have planned for the coming month. Time together ("our time") will be scheduled in the same manner, then, that you schedule business trips or staff meetings.

We realize that at first blush this method may sound formal and mechanical—"a relationship by the numbers"— but it should yield multiple benefits.

First, the marital time map will create a realistic set of expectations about how much time is available for sharing. For many changes, including this one, having appropriate expectations is crucial, for it will minimize the likelihood and the intensity of disappointment. You will not become excited about the prospect of spending a weekend together if you realize that your spouse's Saturdays have been reserved for management development seminars.

Second, a marital time map formalizes both the desire to spend time together and the realization of that desire. It sends a key message to your spouse: "I want to be with you, and, though the demands of work are intense for both of us, I wish to set aside mutually agreeable time and protect it."

Finally, the marital time map forces both partners to sit down and discuss this first major problem in the early career change from working single to working married. It allows them to formulate a method for dealing with the issue of time and the role of work in their lives, to confront problems proactively rather than reactively. When you limit yourself to reacting to a problem, you are more likely to have fewer options and operate under greater stress than when you have antici- pated a difficulty and worked toward its solution.

At the risk of being accused of draining all romance, magic, and spontaneity out of a relationship and treating it as a strategic business planning session, we wish to stress that the marital time map is a guide for conduct, not a strait- jacket. It does not rule out spur-of-the-moment romance, an unplanned rendezvous, a quick lunch, or sudden changes in the map if circumstances change.

Creating Time

Despite the fact that both spouses may have time- demanding jobs, marriage may, ironically, create *more* time for each individual. The key—the "time maker"—is an effec- tive division of labor. There are numerous mindless activities that all people must do simply to maintain their day-to-day existence: shopping for food, going to the dry cleaner, visiting the bank, going to the pharmacy, taking an appliance to be fixed, returning videotapes, *ad nauseam*. Single people typi- cally have to do these tasks by themselves. In a marriage it is necessary for only one partner to undertake each activity for both, so married individuals may *reduce* the time each must spend on such chores.

To achieve an effective division of labor, list the myriad mundane and pedestrian, though time-consuming, activities that must be done each week, and then assign each to you or your spouse. While achieving equity is one consideration, the more important objective is to create leisure time. Tasks should be divided on the basis of who can complete them in the minimum amount of time. If it works out to a 65/35 divi- sion of labor, that should not be seen as a problem. More time together is what you are trying to achieve.

You may also wish to explore the idea of doing home chores together—cooking, gardening, repairing, and clean- ing. While this may seem to fly in the face of the division of labor just described, working together will allow you to share time, complete the tasks in less time, and, perhaps, take some of the drudgery out of house and yard work.

Dealing With The Unexpected

A marital time map and creating time through a division of labor are of little help when the unexpected arises—an important client comes to town unannounced and needs to be entertained; a serious last-minute problem emerges in an advertising campaign; an emergency staff meeting is called. If this necessitates canceling a planned event, both parties should feel free to express their disappointment openly and honestly. Harboring resentment, anger, or guilt will only create additional problems. Reschedule the event or a substitute activity as soon as possible, preferably as soon as you have learned about the disruption. This may mitigate the disappointment the two of you are experiencing and demonstrate your mutual commitment to spending time together.

If an unexpected contingency arises at precisely the time your spouse has a personal or professional problem to discuss, it is probably advisable *not* to tell him or her that you have a few minutes right now since you really *don't*. Rushing through such a conversation, looking and sounding distracted, or short shrifting the problem will create feelings of rejection and hurt rather than empathy and support. Explain that you care about the problem and specify a time when you will be free to sit down and discuss it without pressure and without time limitations.

My Play Time Is No Longer Exclusively *My* Time

Play is too important and too much fun to be the exclusive property of children. It is crucial to preserving one's sanity and equanimity and thus serves a vital function in maintaining a successful working career and a successful marriage.

Yet "play time" and "marriage time" often come into conflict with one another, clashing rather than blending. When this happens, both one's job and one's marriage are adversely affected. Before discussing this conflict, let us consider some of the multiple functions of play for the working person.

Why Play Matters

Playing to relax: Play allows people to decompress after work, to purge themselves of pent-up emotions and hostility, to let the steam out of the pressure cooker (we hope you like mixed metaphors). We all experience days when we come home from work and feel like kicking the dog and screaming at our mates.

We quickly discover, however, that such activities make us *persona non grata*, so we learn to vent our emotions and frustrations in a more socially acceptable and personally effective way: PLAY. Regardless of what form our play time takes— jogging, tennis, aerobics, reading, listening to music—it is difficult to imagine life without it.

Playing to cope: Not only is play beneficial for decompressing after work, it also helps us cope while we're working. Dreams of how we can spend our free time provide us with a momentary mental escape, something to look forward to, an on-the-job retreat that helps us deal with the stresses and frustrations of our work.

Playing for personal control and fulfillment of other needs: Play can offer working people a sense of personal control, individual effectiveness, and attaining desired goals when those needs are not being met at the workplace. An executive who does not receive a promotion he desperately desires may find that he is able to compensate for that disappointment by being elected to the presidency of his local civic association or booster club. An individual who has lost his or her job may find a degree of personal validation in excelling at a sport. Through play we can compensate for a loss, regain our self-esteem, and polish a tarnished ego.

Play may also fulfill other critical human needs that are not satisfied through work. Individuals who work at a solitary job may compensate for working alone by inviting friends out for drinks after work or by belonging to a discussion group. Individuals locked into routine or uncreative jobs may compensate by taking art classes or going to the theater.

Playing to feel human: Finally, play serves as a subtle reminder that we are humans—thinking, feeling organisms possessing creativity, passion, and spontaneity—and not mere robots to be switched on and off at the beginning and end of each work day. These characteristics are plentiful in children, but in our adult world they are quickly replaced by routine, boredom, and predictability

The result in the workplace of losing our sense of creativity, passion, and spontaneity is that we too willingly rely on old solutions to new problems, apply timeworn theories to current issues, resist tackling major projects or taking risks, pour ancient wine into modern bottles. We have learned our lesson well: Stay inside the lines when you color.

Play—adult play—puts us in touch with what is vital and vibrant within us, encourages us to take a chance, to act boldly, to reach beyond our grasp.

Some of the benefits of play that we have described, as well as a potential problem, may be seen in the remarks of a banking executive we interviewed: "I truly love sports. Looking forward to a game is a wonderful way to make it through a gruesome and arduous day on the job. I love watching my favorite teams on the tube or going to Dodger Stadium on a whim. I used to play nine holes of golf in the late afternoon twice a week and 18 holes twice on the weekend. I love the game.

"But I'm married now, and, while I have no regrets, I don't have this freedom anymore. The golf times are fewer and always arranged with my spouse's okay. Every time I gulp that '19th-hole' beer, a twinge of guilt hits me because I think that I should be home with her."

Marriage Isn't Play (This Is News?)

Marriage redefines in part how and when and for how long we carry out these pleasurable activities that help us cope with our jobs and careers. While many couples share play activities, many do not, which often leads to the following kinds of "play time/marriage time" complaints:

> Complaint #1: *"She's so involved with community politics that we typically rush through dinner so that she can get to her smoke-filled room of fellow politicos. She says that local politics is as important to her as her job. She says she loves it, and I can see that she does. But it leaves me feeling like a write-in candidate."*

> Complaint #2: *"When my husband comes home from work, I get the strong, silent treatment. He doesn't want to talk about his day, which is a sure sign that there is something to talk about. Instead he becomes a couch potato, watching anything that has to do remotely with sports, up to and including frog-jumping. In the meantime, I have a million things to talk to him about, and I've got to just swallow them until he feels like talking—which is never."*

> Complaint #3: *"I'm upset about my husband's relationship with the guys at work. This has been going on for about a year—Friday afternoon drinks with his friends that extend into Saturday, talking endlessly on the phone to them, and asking the guys to tag along with us to the movies are typical. I thought it would change after marriage, but he has failed to shift his priorities from them to me. We have little time alone, and I resent it."*

These complaints suggest the complexity and magnitude of the play time/marriage time problem. In Complaint # 1, the wife is obviously fulfilling a number of her needs through her political play activity. Perhaps she receives a level of social support from her colleagues at these meetings that she is not getting at the workplace. The fact that people in political groups are likely to hold similar values, attitudes, and opinions strengthens her feelings of acceptance and affiliation. Perhaps her political activities allow her to exercise a degree of autonomy and to experience personal control, needs which are denied to her at work.

Her play, then, may be crucial to her psychological well-being and to her ability to cope with a less-than-rewarding job. Her husband, of course, feels that his wife is sending him the implicit message, "My political work is more fun, enjoyable, and gratifying than time spent talking to you." While he is protesting another disrupted dinner, she is thinking, "This is the one thing that I do for *me,* and you can't even grant me that. I think it's really selfish of you."

In Complaint # 2, play is being used decompress the tensions of work. It is not unusual for an individual to require some personal and peaceful space and time to unwind after a demanding day. For this husband, television is an escape from the intensity and stress of work into a fantasy world where all problems are solved in 30 or 60 minutes.

His wife, however, uses the opposite method to decompress. Personal interaction, conversation, and communication are her means of putting distance between herself and her job. An unhealthy opposition results: He resents her talking, and she resents his failure to talk. Their frustrations, caused by a lack of mutually acceptable ways to decompress, may carry over into the workplace, negatively impacting the performance of each. Different modes of play and relaxation may undermine their professional as well as their private lives.

Complaint #3 suggests the importance of peer support. As an adolescent looks to his peers in school for approval of his or her actions, values, and beliefs, so will the young adult look for similar support among coworkers. This type of individual is likely to be active in company athletic programs and social events, seeking both the benefit of the activities and the social interaction and moral support of the other participants. Behavior of this nature can fill the journey from working single to working married with potholes and detours, especially if one's spouse has already traveled the same road.

In our composite example, the young husband thinks he has devised a solution in which he can satisfy his need for peer support and his social obligations to his wife by having his buddies and spouse participate in recreational activities together. From the wife's perspective, however, her husband's play interferes with the quality of the time they spend together; she resents the intrusions her husband imposes on her. Their present problems will most likely be exacerbated in the future—unless and until they can devise a means for achieving "our time" instead of "my time."

In selecting appropriate activities for maintaining emotional and psychological well-being, it is important to choose activities that also will allow you to meet the needs of your spouse. To facilitate your choices, both you and your spouse should complete the following section (overlapping answers to the questions are permitted).

Creating Mutual Play Time

Please list in order of importance those play activities that help you reduce the stress and strain of work.

1. _____

2. _____

3. _____

4. _____

Please list in order of importance those play activities that help you to survive an unrewarding or dull day at work.

1._____

2._____

3._____

4._____

Please list in order of importance those play activities that help you fulfill personal needs (e.g., self-esteem, social affiliation, peer support) that you have not been able to fulfill through your job.

1._____

2._____

3._____

4._____

Please list in order of importance those play activities that allow you to feel creative, excited, and spontaneous.

1._____

2._____

3._____

4._____

You and your spouse have now defined and prioritized the types of play that contribute to your sanity and success on the job and in your career. If there is no redundancy among your lists (which is possible, though unlikely), take the play activities from each of your four lists and ask yourself the tie-breaking question: "Which play activity would I be LEAST willing to give up or not engage in as frequently?" That particular play activity represents *your* PRIORITY. Go through this process until you and your spouse have each ranked the top play priorities in your lives.

Now compare lists. Some of the play activities listed by you and your spouse may overlap; this is ideal. The problem areas arise when your play activities are different from or conflict with one another. To resolve this situation, we suggest the following guidelines.

Respect and protect each other's play activities.

You and your spouse now know the key play activities in each other's lives. You also know what work-related functions they serve. It is in your best interest to respect those activities and help each other to protect them. If the husband's priority play activity is, as in the example above, sitting in front of the T.V. and vegetating when he comes home from work, then his wife must respect his need to do this. The wife's awareness of how crucial this is to his ability to cope with the pressures of work should allow her to legitimize this activity in her own mind. It is to be hoped that she will no longer be angered or disappointed by her husband's play activity, for it is now her *expectation* that he will watch television and that both will benefit from the experience.

What happens when the husband's first priority conflicts with his wife's top priority? Mutual adjustment must take place. Perhaps the husband can schedule non-stressful work at the end of his day so that he is less likely to walk through the door emotionally drained and hence be better prepared to converse with his wife about the trials and triumphs of her day. Perhaps he could limit his T.V. viewing to one hour.

Perhaps the wife could engage in activities for that hour—paying bills, making telephone calls, answering mail, writing letters—that would distract her temporarily from the need to discuss her day with her husband. If she enjoys reading, she may want to sit near her husband and read while he watches television; although they are not engaging in the same play or relaxation activities, their physical proximity may create a mutually enjoyable and comfortable atmosphere.

The point is that problems can be solved through mutual adjustment if both spouses are willing to identify their play priorities, understand the vital work-related purposes they serve, and then do what working couples so often fail to do: talk to one another about their feelings.

Schedule play time just like "our time."

In the same manner that you scheduled your time together ("our time") into your marital time map, schedule your play time. Doing so helps to protect play from being intruded upon by competing activities. It also will allow you to schedule separate play (i.e., play not mutually engaged in by husband and wife) at concurrent times. If a wife's political meetings, for instance, are on Tuesday evenings, her husband may schedule that same time for his tennis match or poker game.

Disappointments and emotional letdowns should be minimized, for each person will know beforehand when the other plans to fulfill his or her individual play needs. Furthermore, if one spouse feels that he or she is paying too great a price for the other's play, programming will allow each party to examine the problem and work on a mutual adjustment to resolve it.

Evaluate and re-evaluate the adjustments you've made.

We recommend that at least four times a year both spouses evaluate how well (or poorly) their play activities are enhancing their work life and whether their adjustments to each other's priorities have been effective and equitable. You may wish to consider the following questions as a starting point:

- Are both of you focusing on play that has a highly beneficial effect? Or is less important play—play that has a relatively low work- and pleasure-related value—confounding your scheduling?
- Is the scheduling of play into the marital time map working effectively?

- Is one of you making an inordinate amount of adjustments for the other?
- Is there a mutually acceptable balance between "my time" and "our time?"

Married Time Versus Work Time And Play Time

The third major problem in making the change from working single to working married involves managing the many new demands that will now be made on your time, patience, and energy simply because you have entered into a state of wedded bliss.

How Nice. Aunt Martha's Coming...Again

As a couple you will now have to face a totally new set of time and energy demands that compete directly with both your work time and play time. One does not simply take a spouse for better or worse; one also takes the family and friends of the spouse for better or worse. The genuine excitement felt by family and friends over a marriage often manifests itself in their desire to spend time with the newlyweds.

The temporal demands on the new couple can be overwhelming. Initially you may try to be all things to all people, but you will quickly learn that it is impossible to spend a great deal of time with your extended family and friends while trying to maintain "my time" and "our time" and "work time" and "play time." The following complaints may all too soon sound familiar:

Complaint #1: *"What do you mean I can't go to the football game with the guys this Sunday? How do you think I made it through a dull week of inventory control? I've been looking forward*

*to this all week! Your parents visit us enough as
it is. They'll understand, won't they?"*

Complaint #2: *"I don't mind getting home early
from work to be with you, but I do mind giving
up three hours of work time in order to go out
with your friend Michael and his dull wife. She
always makes me feel guilty that I want a
career instead of a family. I don't want to go!"*

Complaint #3: *"This is getting ridiculous. We
both work, see very little of each other as it is,
and then you spend the whole night on the
phone talking to your parents. It's not fair."*

Now the good news: You already have a mechanism to
solve these transitional problems. The marital time map may
now be used to factor in your family responsibilities and social
obligations. Your priority list of play activities may be expanded to include pursuits that involve extended families and
friends. Mutual adjustment, programming, and evaluation
also will be necessary. In addition, you may wish to consider
the following suggestions:

- If you live at a distance from your parents or in-
  laws and feel obligated to see them, suggest *they*
  visit *you*. You may wish to consider having your
  parents and in-laws visit at the same time—maybe
  they'll entertain each another. But remember Ben-
  jamin Franklin's remark: "Fish and house guests
  both smell after three days."

- Cards, letters, or brief phone calls are less time
  consuming than home visits and dinners out.
  Friendships and family relations can be successfully maintained by emphasizing these methods.

- Newlyweds need not feel obligated to interact with
  all—or even their favorite—family members and
  friends during the first weeks or months of marriage. Activities with them can be stretched out
  over a period of time that feels comfortable to both of
  you.

- Your work is a legitimate and socially acceptable reason to delay seeing family and friends or to decline invitations from them.

- Your spouse's work is a legitimate and socially acceptable reason to delay seeing friends and family or to decline invitations from them.

- Being married does not mean that you have to do everything in tandem. The division-of-labor principle should be invoked when appropriate. It is not necessary, for instance, for your spouse to speak to your mother every time she calls.

- Remember that your spouse married *you,* not your family and network of friends. While not disregarding these people, you should have no difficulty determining who should be the primary recipient of your time and energy.

Whose Career Comes First?

The Scenario: You cannot believe what happened at the office today. The president of the company, whom you have met by photograph only (even though you have worked at the firm for three years), walked into your office unannounced.

After embarrassing yourself by calling him "Mr. President," and pouring your coffee on your lap, you asked him to sit down. With a voice resembling Charleton Heston in "The Ten Commandments," he made you an incredible offer: Since you had been doing such magnificent work for the firm, he wanted you to move from Des Moines, Iowa, to Atlanta, Georgia, to open up a new health insurance division. Your title would go from "Assistant Nothing" to "Vice-President, Division of Health Care Underwriting." Your salary would be commensurate with your new responsibilities—a cool six figures. To sweeten the pot, a car, subsidized housing, and a stock option plan would be thrown in.

Somehow you managed to suppress the urge to kiss his feet and promise him your first born. Breathing deeply, you mustered enough composure to say, "The offer sounds great, and I am honored. But I have to talk it over with my husband. He, too, has a career that is very important to him."

He nodded understandingly and said that you had one week to decide what you were going to do.

In today's mobile and flourishing workplace, this scenario is not unusual. Sometimes it is the husband who is faced with a career opportunity that would require his wife to move. Either way, it is one of the toughest problems to be confronted in the working single/working married transition.

The permutations, contingencies, unknowns, and unpredictables are likely to leave one talking to oneself: Can my spouse find an equally good job in a new location? What if he tries and cannot? Will he resent me for pushing him to leave? How will this affect his family, who will now be separated from him by 2,000 miles? What if the new job blows up in my face? What if I never get this chance again? Should I wait for a similar opportunity with less risk? Am I ready for such a move? Will my company penalize me for not taking the new job? And so on.

While the multitude of uncertainties over this new opportunity is difficult enough to cope with, the emotional and personal implications and consequences intensify the stress until it becomes almost unbearable. The husband, for example, wants to give his wife a free choice, but at the same time he is scared to death of giving up his secure job. The wife does not want to force her husband into a decision about which he has misgivings, yet she is dying to take the new job. Each does not want to stand in the other's way, yet each wants to protect his or her self-interests. A solid, stable relationship has suddenly become a ticking career time bomb.

Many of the potential problems, as well as the nail biting inherent in making a career decision that requires relocating, may be minimized by following several guidelines and considering a variety of obvious and not-so-obvious issues.

Decision-Making Guidelines

Try for a win-win scenario, but don't expect to attain it.

It would be ideal if both spouses found jobs superior to their current employment. This, however, is rarely the case. When working couples move, it usually means that one person will be making either a descending or a lateral move. On the positive side, the cost to this individual will probably lessen over time. But a key to successful job or career transitions is to base your expectations on reality, not wishful thinking.

Make the move if comparability can be established.

If one spouse is offered a wonderful new job that he or she badly wants, and if the trailing spouse is fortunate enough to secure a position *comparable* to the one he or she currently holds, then the decision to move seems advisable.

The desire to recruit effectively has led an increasing number of major firms across the country to initiate spousal relocation programs to assist the "trailing" spouse in his or her pursuit of suitable employment. If your new company does not offer such a program, you may, nonetheless, be able to negotiate some sort of corporate support for your spouse. Such support may range from financial assistance to use of company resources (e.g., job placement services, clerical help) in pursuing employment.

Determine if the career of one spouse is more important to you as a couple than the other's.

If it is mutually agreed that the career of the person receiving the offer is more important to your collective welfare and happiness than the other's career, then the decision to move seems advisable. Under these circumstances, the trailing spouse should be supportive, even if there are short-term costs to him or her.

Factor opportunity costs into your decision.

Opportunity costs are the losses suffered by *not* making an alternative decision. Here are the things to keep in mind:

1) If the job offer is clearly a "once in a lifetime" opportunity, take the new job. The opportunity costs of
   turning it down are probably too high.

2) You may be penalized by some companies if you do
   not accept their offer of a better job at a new location.
   They may view this refusal as a sign of low corporate commitment or even disloyalty and never offer
   you a similar opportunity. Since the opportunity
   costs of turning down an offer in this context are
   high, it is probably advisable to accept, assuming, of
   course, that you are able to fulfill the task interest
   and goal satisfaction rules we discussed in the Success Equation in chapter 1.

3) If the new job offers only a slight change for the better, and turning it down incurs no penalties, there
   is little reason to accept it. When you consider the
   cost of making a physical move, combined with the
   challenges of readjustment and "proving yourself"
   all over again, the opportunity costs of relocating are
   probably greater than maintaining the status quo.

The concept of opportunity costs is largely a financial way
of evaluating a potential job move. If a move is advisable in
terms of its opportunity costs (contingencies 1 and 2) but your
spouse would suffer a clear and significant loss, we would
advise against the move. No alternative job or career opportunity is worth taking if it is likely to make one's spouse so
miserable that it would tarnish the quality of his or her life
and your relationship.

We urge both spouses, however, to be creative and flexible
in looking for ways to minimize the negative impact of a move
on the trailing individual. Aside from the obvious strategy of
finding him or her a comparable position, there are several
stop-gap measures that should be considered:

• Traveling from the new location to your present
  home to be with your spouse on weekends;

• Working extra hours during the week so that you
  may spend long weekends with your spouse;

- Relocating the job offer to where you are currently living (a long shot at best);
- Counter-offering to the company a similar job opportunity that would not necessitate moving;
- Negotiating with the company a package deal in which they take both spouses.

These suggestions can be augmented by your own ideas. We urge you, however, not to throw in the towel prematurely —leave no stone unturned to find an imaginative or subtle solution.

Factor in the intangibles.

Relocating often means more than simply leaving a job—it may mean leaving family and friends, a home and community about which you care, and all that is familiar and thus comforting to you. The overall effect of this differs greatly among individuals, but its impact on both spouses should be carefully considered.

Consider, for instance, the case of an executive we interviewed who was offered a new job in a slightly more prestigious company, a salary increase of roughly 100%, similar work responsibilities, and an equally high rank in the organization (he was already an executive vice-president). The move would necessitate leaving his current job in New York and relocating to Wisconsin. This was an excellent offer, and he agonized over his decision.

Ultimately, he rejected the offer. He did so, he averred, for six reasons: (1) He liked the work he was currently doing and saw no gains to be made in terms of task interest and goal satisfaction. (2) His wife's family was from New York, and both he and his spouse wished to remain near them. (3) He liked his colleagues in his current firm a great deal. (4) Two of his children were in high school, and he did not want to disrupt their social network or the continuity of their education. (5) He felt a strong religious and emotional attachment to his local church. (6) He thought his current salary was adequate for his needs.

To make decisions of this nature even more difficult than they inherently are, you will occasionally be confronted with a job offer in which the positives and negatives balance one another, leaving you in deathly equilibrium. What if you determine that your career is more important than your spouse's and that this is a "once in a lifetime opportunity," but you know that your spouse will be absolutely miserable in the new location, will miss his or her family, and that the move could tarnish your relationship with your spouse?

The tie-breaking principle is that people are more important than careers. The greatest career move in history is not worth taking if it will make your spouse absolutely miserable. Your commitment to your spouse should take precedence over your commitment to your job and career.

One final caveat: While decisions of this type require rational analysis, it is difficult and probably not desirable to be totally analytical and coolly objective in your deliberations. Decisions of this nature are made in the heart as well as in the head.

Better yet, they are made in two hearts and in two heads.

The Positive Side
Of Working Married

We have dwelled throughout this chapter on the *difficulties* posed by the transition from working single to working married. So as not to be accused of misogamy, let us add that we believe the greatest single asset one can have in pursing a career is an understanding and supportive spouse.

A spouse can provide assistance that is as varied as it is important. When you have reached a dead end trying to resolve an issue at work, your spouse can offer an objective assessment and analysis.

When you need to practice a major sales presentation or wish to get a second opinion on a marketing report you have written, your spouse can serve as a trial audience and critic.

When you need honest feedback, your spouse can be one of the most reliable sources you can find. In fact, we know of many business and academic professionals who would not dream of making a major decision without first soliciting the advice of their spouses.

Spouses can also serve a vital social function in the workplace by helping to entertain clients and colleagues and accompanying their mates to business conferences and work-related social functions.

Most careers involve failures as well as successes, disappointment as well as fulfillment, valleys as well as peaks. Having another person who cares about your welfare to share your confusion and frustration, to listen to your fears and anxieties, and to provide you with counsel as well as comfort is a blessing that cannot be surpassed. When one loses a huge account, fails to get a promotion that is deserved, receives a poor performance appraisal, or is fired from a job, a spouse can restore self-esteem, rebuild confidence, and lend moral support.

Most importantly, a spouse can provide a sense of balance and a broad perspective on oneself and one's problems, for he or she is a living reminder of what is truly important in life. And what only *seems* important at the moment.

Epilogue

WE HOPE YOU
ENJOY THE JOURNEY!

Throughout **FROM CAMPUS TO CORPORATION And The Next Ten Years,** we have endeavored to help you find your first job after graduation, to succeed at it, and to lay the groundwork for a fulfilling future.

A number of major themes have emerged from our discussions, themes that will run throughout you working life.

Self-Knowledge

The starting point for all knowledge is self-knowledge—to know your talents and tastes, your predilections and prejudices, your failings and foibles. To know what wakes you up and what puts you to sleep. What gives you a sense of fulfillment and what leaves you with a sense of emptiness.

Self-knowledge is vital at all stages of your career: To recognize an entry-level job that will fit your talents and goals; to know when it is time to change jobs; to understand when you should try harder and when you should back off; to recognize the stereotypes and preconceived notions of people and jobs that you carry with you; to realize your personal foibles and how they will affect your ability to live harmoniously with a spouse; to confront the anxieties you may have about the future; to know why you like and dislike certain types of bosses.

If self-knowledge will bring the career traveler to the oasis that he or she seeks, *self-deception* is a deadly mirage. There are few—if any—types of dishonesty more harmful than to try to be someone you are not, and to convince yourself that this artificial pose is the true reality. If you are to adjust to the new opportunities and challenges brought on by change, you must first make an honest appraisal of yourself, alter what you think can and should be altered, accept what cannot be changed, and love the person who emerges—warts and all.

Knowledge Of The Workplace

A major theme running throughout **FROM CAMPUS TO CORPORATION** is that the success of your job and career changes will depend on how well you understand your working environment. When you begin a new job, it is critical to know how to "read" your boss, how to stay in touch with your clients and customers, how to learn the culture and reward systems of your firm, how to evaluate your work, and how to determine if you are acting ethically.

Honest And Objective Evaluation

This may be considered a sub-theme of knowing yourself. For job and career change to be managed successfully, it is vital to determine the precise demands of your new job or role, what skills you must develop, and how you will go about meeting those demands and acquiring the requisite skills. At times you will have to add to your workplace repertoire—developing, for instance, a different leadership style or learning how to work for a person of different gender. At times you will be required to make major changes in your attitudes or modes of behavior—adjusting to the demands of the workplace after becoming married.

To succeed in the present and plan for the future also demands that you evaluate and understand what has happened in the past and resolve any lingering problems. Only by coming to terms with unpleasant experiences you may have had with a particular boss, a certain type of work, or in your personal life, only by putting to rest those public and private ghosts, can you flourish in the present and the future.

Growth

Transitions and the person experiencing them have a reciprocal influence. The individual puts his or her particular stamp on the new job or new role, while the transition shapes and molds the individual. The non-manager who suddenly becomes a manager must now learn to delegate work, even though he or she has been accustomed to completing work alone. The new female employee may have to learn to function without peer support. The fired employee must develop the perseverance to "work" at home to find a new job.

Transitions deny you the comforts of complacency and the status quo. Transitional survival compels you to develop new professional skills, explore fresh modes of personal behavior, remain on the cutting edge, and discover and awaken dormant talents. Transitions provoke, excite, challenge, and stimulate you to reach the full measure of your potential.

Resources

Fortunately, you are not alone when making a job or career transition—there are numerous resources at your disposal. Professional publications in your particular field; articles and books (such as the one you are now reading) that offer guidance and advice on the workplace in general; colleagues, friends, and family who can provide assistance, from helping you role play an interview and providing you with job leads to offering advice on management styles.

Ultimately, however, as we have suggested throughout this book, you are your own best resource. It is your courage, tenacity, patience, ambition, desire, and willingness to learn over an entire lifetime that will determine your level of success and personal well-being.

Planning

We hope that reading **FROM CAMPUS TO CORPORATION** has convinced you that it is prudent and profitable to regularly look beyond the mountain of memos and reports, projects and projections, stacked on your desk and to confront the future. Positioning yourself for a management job, devising strategies to avoid being fired, balancing marriage and work, all require careful and systematic planning.

Change is constant. It will occur with or without your consent. And if you wish to maximize the opportunities that it brings, you must think and plan beyond the present.

Impact On Others

Transitions rarely affect only the person experiencing them—they have a centrifugal force that is constantly reaching out to touch others. Some transitions are immediately recognized as having a potentially profound impact on family and friends: starting full-time employment, changing jobs or careers, being fired or laid off, getting married.

Other transitions may seem innocuous on the surface— receiving a promotion to a managerial position, working for a new boss, learning the culture of a new firm. Yet these latter transitions may very well carry with them an explosive mixture—tension, anxiety, depression, withdrawal, frustration— and it is unlikely that the fallout will not be felt by the individual's family and friends.

It is important for all parties to realize that one's work life and personal life are intertwined, and that they should be sympathetic to the emotional, psychological, and even physical manifestations of change. Transitions demand sensitivity and support, kindness and patience, compassion and understanding. They are major life events that should, hopefully, bring out the best in all of us.

Work

Job and career transition and change, by definition, mean disturbing the status quo, leaving the old and taking on the new—new responsibilities, new roles, new challenges, new ways of looking at your work and yourself. None of this comes without hard and disciplined work—and lots of it.

We do not, however, offer you sympathy, for work is not simply a means to an end—it is a wonderful and meaningful end in itself. Writer Joseph Conrad said that he did not like work. What he liked was what was *in* the work: the opportunity it gave him to find himself.

Fun

One recurring theme in this book is that work and change can and should be the source of pleasure and enjoyment. When work becomes routine—when we can perform tasks facilely because we have done them so often—we run the risk of becoming mechanical people bored with life.

Change is an effective antidote to *ennui*. Change stimulates us and keeps us vital and dynamic. It allows us to renew and revivify ourselves, to find the excitement in our work and, ultimately, in ourselves that we experienced when we undertook a task for the first time.

Perhaps we can expand Joseph Conrad's statement to read that work not only allows us to find ourselves, but also to experience the delight and enjoyment that reside in the process of self-discovery.

Index

5510